Heaven Is a
Beautiful Place

Heaven Is a Beautiful Place

A Memoir of the South Carolina Coast

Genevieve C. Peterkin

In conversation with

William P. Baldwin

University of South Carolina Press

Published in Columbia, South Carolina, by the
University of South Carolina Press

Manufactured in the United States of America

04 03 02 01   5 4 3

Library of Congress Cataloging-in-Publication Data

Peterkin, Genevieve C. (Genevieve Chandler), 1928–
    Heaven is a beautiful place : a memoir of the South Carolina coast /
Genevieve C. Peterkin in conversation with William P. Baldwin.
       p. cm.
    ISBN 1-57003-361-7 (alk. paper)
       1. Peterkin, Genevieve C. (Genevieve Chandler), 1928– 2. Murrells
Inlet (S.C.)—Biography. I. Baldwin, William P. II. Title.
CT275.P5815 A3 2000
975.7'87—dc21   00-008174

This book contains excerpts from interviews conducted by Genevieve Willcox Chandler
for the Federal Writer's Project of the Works Progress Administration. The interviews
are among the collections of the Library of Congress and the South Caroliniana Library,
University of South Carolina.

Contents

Introduction

THIS IS A WONDERFUL BOOK. But I can't claim that was my original intention. At the start I approached seventy-year-old Genevieve Chandler Peterkin (known to most as "Sister") to suggest we collaborate on a story collection. I had in mind assorted tales, ghost stories, and what-not mixed with some bits of her own life—a glimpse of the South Carolina seacoast and, in particular, of the Murrells Inlet community where she was born and raised.

Murrells Inlet was an entertaining enough little corner of the world, and Sister had a reputation as a storyteller, one which I knew from experience was well deserved. I had known her for at least fifteen years, and we enjoyed each other's company. A quick book project seemed simple enough. I planned to visit her handsome old home and tape-record her for two hours each week. I would eat pound cake and drink coffee and keep my back to the window and its distracting marsh vista. She would speak into the microphone. That would be the book.

But at the end of the second session she said, "Billy, I want this to be about my son." Her son, Jim, had been killed in a boating accident when he was twenty. I knew that much. She still wanted to entertain people—which she does here and does handily. But at the same time she wanted to say something that mattered—and not just about her son. She wanted to say something about the South—the beautiful, romantic, friendly, and self-reliant South and also the other South, the warts-and-all South, and she wanted to talk about striving to serve the common good and about loving people and losing the people you love. She wanted to say that this is what it means to be a caring human being. The result is what you hold in your hand.

Two-thirds of the way into the project Patty Fulcher, who was transcribing the tapes, asked to join us in the two-hour recording sessions. She had lost a child under similar circumstances and understood far better than I what Sister was attempting. Though I was in the room, that section of the conversation entitled "Jim" was spoken directly to Patty. Thank you, Patty.

And now, reader, I present to you a life—a warm, funny, sad, rich and raw and honest account. Each time I read through this manuscript I'm staggered by its power. God bless Sister.

William Baldwin

Two Worlds

Little Red Horses

LILLIE KNOX FRIED CORN BREADS she called her Little Red Horses, and the hush puppies of this present time don't compare in any way. She fried them on a flat iron griddle with not much grease. They were an inch thick and she'd flip them like pancakes, and when they were golden red brown they went on our plates. This was during the Depression. We had seafood, but meat was a rare treat after Daddy died, and I have the clearest memory of being at the kitchen table, asking Lillie for meat to go with my field peas and rice, and her answering "Darling, my little red horses is what you get today."

In my own heart I always had two mothers, because Lillie Knox was always there. This black woman was such a warm and sweet and loving person. Of course, my white Mama was there too, but Lil was plump and I could crawl up on her lap. That was the most comfortable place in the world to be, especially if I'd stumped a toe or had my feelings hurt.

Lillie always had on a clean white apron. She pressed our clothes with an old flat iron that had to be heated on the wood stove. She would go into the yard and break off a branch of a cedar, a branch with blue berries growing on it, or she got berries off a myrtle tree. Then she ran that black iron over those waxy berries from the cedar or myrtle so everything she pressed just smelled wonderful. Such a clean scent.

Back at the beginning there were only my mama and daddy, my older sister, June, and my infant brother Tommy and me—who was named Genevieve for my mother but called "Little Sister." My two youngest brothers hadn't been born yet, so those first four of my family were the only white people in my life. We were living in a cottage at Wachesaw, which was a portion of an old plantation and a riverboat

landing. Yes, they still had riverboats in those distant days of the early
1930s—paddlewheel steamboats. We were about five miles inland from
the seashore community of Murrells Inlet, South Carolina, and except
for our black neighbors we were very cut off for most of the time. I was
literally in a black world, and as a child I must have gotten things pretty
confused. Mama talked about Lillie's grandmother, Aunt Kit, and hearing the word *Aunt,* my childhood mind became very confused about
who was my aunt by blood and who wasn't. Now, Mama said that Lillie's
Aunt Kit had long, straight, black hair and sort of greenish-gray eyes
and a reddish cast to her skin, more bronzy than black. So when I was
in the third grade I think I invented the first Show and Tell. We were
studying South Carolina history in a little country schoolhouse and
learning about the Indians along this part of the coast. I didn't tell
Mama but I took her tomahawk, her best tomahawk.

She had quite a collection of Indian artifacts. At Wachesaw we would
follow the plowmen and pick up arrowheads and all kinds of pottery.
This high bluff on the river had obviously been the site of an Indian settlement. Anyway, I took Mama's finest tomahawk, which was actually a
stone axe. On a thread she had strung beads taken from the Indian
graves at Wachesaw (the graves are a subject to which I'll be returning).
I took those beads and some pottery game pieces. I sort of went among
Mama's relics and took what I wanted to school and showed them in
my class.

Now, I had very dark brown eyes and very long dark brown hair
that I wore in two long pigtails down to my waist, so I probably looked
as much Indian as Lillie's grandmother. And I stood up in front of my
third grade class and told them that the beads belonged to my grandmother. I didn't mean to be telling a lie. I thought that was the truth.
About two months later Mama came to school for something and my
teacher Mrs. Sanders said, "Mrs. Genevieve, I didn't know you all were
Indians." Mama said, "What?" By then it was all over the community
about how my grandmother had the long black straight hair and the
greenish-gray eyes.

I guess I'm telling you this up front not just because it marks my beginnings but so you will understand how closely connected I felt at that age to this black woman Lillie Knox—how completely intertwined my young life was with hers. You see, a much earlier memory I have of her concerns the Indian graves. I was five, maybe six years old. My grandfather had owned Wachesaw plantation but he'd had to sell it. The new owner was a wealthy and generous Northerner named Mr. William A. Kimbel who kept my daddy on as a caretaker. The Kimbels would only come down for brief times in the winter to hunt ducks. Mr. Kimbel asked my daddy to build him a log cabin on the banks of the river right where the retirement community Wachesaw Plantation now has its river-view restaurant. When Daddy was digging the foundation the crew dug into Indian graves. The first grave held thirteen skeletons of young women all in sitting positions. And in the second grave they found the skeleton of a mother holding her baby in her lap. She had been buried seated, and her arms were still holding the skeleton of that baby. They thought she had died in childbirth, but the thirteen young women in the first grave were equally fascinating to the archaeologists who came from the Charleston Museum and even the Smithsonian Institution to investigate. An epidemic was considered the most likely cause of those deaths, and one translation of Wachesaw is "Place of the Great Weeping."

Anyway, I was just five years old and Mama and Daddy were gone from the house, leaving me with Lillie Knox. Lillie came every day to take care of my sister, June, and me and the baby—to watch us and to cook and do everything a person could to be of help. Lillie was in the kitchen so Mama was free to go and sift dirt with the archaeologists. She and Daddy stayed down at those graves.

Lillie, as I just mentioned, had a grandmother called Aunt Kit, who though a former slave was mostly Indian—the straight-haired, green-eyed woman. And Aunt Kit was on Lillie's mind, for she was mumbling and grumbling as she washed up the dishes in the sink. And from all this mumbling and grumbling I realized Lillie was terribly disturbed that they were digging in these graves and removing bones from them.

Quite rightly, she felt that the graves of Indians were just as sacred as those of everyone else.

I listened and then, taking along a cardboard box, snuck out to the site. The archaeologists had stopped for the afternoon, but they'd left skeletons laid out on the ground, and my plan was to compensate for what my Mama and Daddy and these scientists were doing—for the destruction of these graves. I didn't get a whole Indian, but I did get a skull and a number of bones which I took well up the bluff to a big live oak tree. And in the vee of a root I dug a shallow hole and buried at least a portion of an Indian. From that time on I called that little spot the "happy hunting ground" and decorated it with wildflowers in a Mason jar.

Many years later my son, Jim, got interested in Indian artifacts. He went over to big Lake Marion when the water was low and made some incredible finds. I'd told him about burying the Indian skeleton, and he asked if he could dig it up. But I didn't think Mrs. Kimbel would appreciate that. Then many years later when they were turning Wachesaw into a resort, an archaeologist named James Michie called me, for he'd heard that a little girl died with diphtheria when those graves were opened in the 1930s and he'd been told I might know something about that since my father was the manager. I said, "Well, she didn't die. I'm that little girl." Then I met Jim Michie and showed him where I'd buried the Indian bones. We became great friends. He dug between the roots of the tree and found nothing, which hardly surprised me since that 1934 tree had spread out considerably.

As for diphtheria, I did catch it, and apparently the disease did come from my handling those bones that I'd buried or at least was connected to the digging in some way. When I got sick, they decided that the graves had germs and told Mama and Daddy to fumigate our whole house. Daddy moved us over to the Hermitage, my grandparents' house at the Inlet. They told him to get sulfur candles and burn them in the house for twenty-four hours. They said to run clotheslines through the house and hang up all the woolen bedding and woolen clothes. Anything that couldn't be washed thoroughly had to be fumigated along with the house. So Daddy ran these lines through the house, and from Old Man Eason's store he bought metal dishpans which he filled with sand. And the sulfur candles went in the middle of the sand. All this to be safe. Then he took Mama and us children over to the Hermitage and left somebody to watch the fumigating. During the night that person fell asleep and the house burned down.

What really made this sad was that Daddy's father and mother had both died the previous year, and only three weeks before the fire Daddy had brought all the furniture he had inherited to our house. You know when a person has had a fire—well, I know this from living with Mama and with my husband, both of whom lost houses with everything in them. For the rest of her life Mama would occasionally say, "Sis, have you seen my something or another?" And I'd say, "Mama, I never saw it in my life." "Oh," she would say, "I lost that in the fire at Wachesaw." Mama and Daddy had hired a truck and brought all that furniture down here from his old home in Williamsburg County—irreplaceable things—and belongings from my mother's side of the family had gone as well. Daddy did build a house on the same foundation though—pretty much the same house: a cottage with a screened porch across half the front and an open porch on the rest and with a chimney at each end.

All this happened when I was barely six. Two years later when I went to school loaded down with beads and tomahawk and claiming to have an Indian grandmother, well, that attachment to Lillie and her Indian grandmother had already been forged in what I could call a fiery furnace. In my heart I truly did have those two mothers—Mama and Lillie Knox. And in all the years since, I guess, I have been straddling those two worlds, the white and the black. I was born in the first, but I've always been borrowing strengths from the other. And as you're about to see, we do need all the strengths and comforts we can get.

I guess you could say the following is what Lillie and Mama taught me—what they taught me about faith, courage, and love. And I'm going to tell you the story of my son, Jim, who died when he was twenty. When my son died I couldn't cry, not really. I had so much else

on me, my husband and mother both ill. Oh, but tears are so important. Memories can make you cry. You can even cry for joy. Sometimes
it just comes to me—I'm really finally crying.

Mama

My mama, Genevieve Willcox Chandler, was the only white woman around Murrells Inlet who would catch stone crabs with just her bare hand. You have to put your arm down in the hole. A stone crab is a bit like a lobster. The body is only four or five inches across, and it has one small claw. And it has one giant claw that can be as big as the rest of the crab put together. Now, we have five feet of tide along here. At high tide the water rises and the creek brims over and leaves just the tip of the marsh showing. At low tide the water falls, leaving the mudflats and oyster banks exposed and glistening. This is when you gather oysters and clams—and the stone crabs too, if you have the courage.

Mama could take them, but it was the one thing I wouldn't even try. She told me exactly how, but I just wasn't brave enough. A stone crab makes a long tunnel down into the oyster rock, and this tunnel is well below the water level at that dead low tide. You can see the fresh shell that the old stone crab breaks off all around the entrance, and he is waiting at the bottom of that tunnel. This tunnel is always about an arm's length long, and what you do—I mean an expert does this but I can't—is you make your hand very stiff and keep your fingers very stiff. You start and run your hand right along the roof of the hole, and when you feel his back it's going to feel very smooth. He's always facing forward with his giant claw tucked up in front. You feel his back, you crook your fingers over it, and then you snatch him quick. Or he gets you.

But if you snatch quick enough, that's all there is to it. He's out of the hole. You break off the big claw and let him go, and the little claw will grow to be the dominant one. But if you mess this up he can easily break one or more of your fingers, and there are even nightmare stories of people being held with their arms in the hole until the rising tide drowns them. And Mama did get bitten one time. She said she was lucky because the claw caught her in the fleshy part between the thumb and forefinger and her brother Dick was with her. She said, "He said, Sis, just relax, just relax, keep still and relax." So she lay there stretched out on the oyster rock with her arm down in the hole for quite a while and finally she felt the crab release her. She snatched her hand out, and Bubba Dick said if you don't go back and get that crab you'll never do it again. He made her stiffen her hand and go right back in and catch that animal. I suppose *make* isn't the right word. He encouraged her. He made her understand that if she didn't face her fear right then she probably never would.

Mama had actually grown up in Marion, South Carolina, which is a pretty little town about sixty miles in from the coast, but her father had discovered Murrells Inlet, which he rightly called "the garden of Eden." He would bring his family here to vacation, and finally they settled permanently and were living in an old plantation house called the Hermitage. When she was fourteen Mama went off to a little Presbyterian college in North Carolina, Flora MacDonald, and after two years there she spent two years at the Art Students League in New York. Then she came home.

Mama was eighteen when her parents moved here to Murrells Inlet. The following year she started teaching school in nearby Collins Creek. She rode horseback from the Hermitage to that school, where she taught all eight grades in one classroom. She was the only teacher. She told me she always carried a pistol. Mama was very good with a rifle, but she always carried a pistol through that six miles of wilderness. She said the only things she was afraid of were rattlesnakes and drunk men. She never had to shoot anything but a rattlesnake.

I heard a tale of those days not so long ago. Herman Wilson told his daughter he'd never forget his first day of school with Miss Genevieve. Mama was quite petite, and even the sixth grade boys were taller than she. Mr. Wilson said that first day Miss Genevieve came down the aisle, turned and faced them, reached in her pocket, and took out a pistol which she laid on the desk. "Now, boys," she said, "I know I won't have any trouble with you this year." I expect she was just getting the word out that she was armed.

But once she did say that the meanest thing she ever did in her life was at that Collins Creek School. A creek ran right by the school windows, and she couldn't keep the boys' attention because a mother deer with a little spotted fawn was drinking from the creek or some other wildlife distraction was going on outside. She knew those boys were dreaming of hunting so she took a bucket of paint and painted over the glass in the lower half of all the windows.

I know she made a big difference in those children's lives, but she also realized pretty quickly that many of these children's parents were illiterate. White people, of course. A totally white school. Mama decided to go back at night and teach the parents, and her mother rode with her. They used a buggy at night. Mama said Granny would make coffee and doughnuts and haul them to the school. Mama said people came for the refreshments and stayed to learn a little. And they did make a difference. They truly did. Sixty years later when I worked in the polls an amazing number of people told me they didn't have to make a mark for a signature. They'd say, "I can sign my name 'cause your mama taught me how." And some of the people who said that were black, because during the same period Mama was doing adult education for blacks in the kitchen of the Hermitage.

Another project that Mama and Granny undertook back then still gets an occasional mention today. Around 1912 they put on what might have been the first outdoor drama ever staged on the East Coast. To make money for a school playground Granny took Longfellow's poem *Hiawatha* and wrote a script. All winter long the local families, both children and parents, came to the Hermitage. Granny gave out the speaking parts early so the actors could be studying, and the rest were sewing costumes. All the tin foil out of men's cigarette packages got saved to make glitter for the costumes. Also they used sea shells. Basically, the seamstresses were decorating croker sacks. When *Hiawatha* was finally put on, people were amazed. Mama had an uncle who was a railway attorney and often traveled. He said, "Genevieve, how in the world did you find a costume house in New York to do all this?" Quite a compliment.

They always gave that play on the full moon in June because they needed the light of the moon and they needed the high water. In the end Hiawatha sailed away in his canoe. Men and boys hid out on a little shell midden and held onto a cable that ran inshore to the canoe. Hiawatha could just step into that canoe, raise his arms in the air, and glide out with the full moon in the background because the men and boys were gently tugging him out. One old man always told Mama how much he resented the *Hiawatha* production because his family—wife and children—would be at the Hermitage every Friday night working on that play. And confusing the Indian name with the setting, he'd call it "that damn old 'High Water.'"

In 1913 Mama went to Liverpool, England, and studied portrait painting. Then she returned home again and taught school until we entered World War I. The YWCA selected two young women from every state to send overseas, and Mama was chosen and attached to the Rainbow Division. Col. Monroe Johnson, who also grew up in Marion, was her dear friend and commanding officer. Of course, Mama was a civilian. They were called YWCA Hostesses and were a forerunner of the Special Services, the same group I was a librarian with after World War II. She was stationed first in France and then in Germany during the occupation. They made and served doughnuts and coffee for the men, wrote letters for them, and arranged for money orders to be sent home to wives, that sort of thing.

Both her brothers were already over there with the Rainbow Division, and my father was with that division as well, but he didn't meet Mama until after the war. I don't know that Mama actually saw much of Europe. The hostesses weren't given much opportunity to tour. Once she attended a big dinner in a castle in Cologne, and that impressed her. And she saw General Pershing in Paris. When I was a child she still had her uniform with its beautiful rainbow patch, but that disappeared somewhere along the line.

But long before the war Mama had been out in the world. She'd spent those two years in New York in the Art Students League. She had a professor there named Dumas who was quite famous, and if he felt your drawing was perfect he would initial it with a D on the bottom— a way of saying he wouldn't be embarrassed to claim it for his own. The year was 1910, and this was figure drawing. She did all these beautiful charcoal drawings and all were nude—both men and women. She must have been really shocked as a young woman to arrive from a little Presbyterian college like Flora MacDonald where they were still studying Gaelic and John Calvin—to go from that to New York and sketching the nude models.

Those sketches were in the attic at the Hermitage, and my sister, June, is a cleaner. I'm a clutterer. When June was around twenty she married; and she married a Yankee, which only made her worse about cleaning house. Her husband Ken was a wonderful man. I can honestly say that he and my sister, June, were and will always be two of my closest friends, but Ken and June together would go around like a whirlwind and whirl until they had established order. They cleaned up the attic. I guess June was twenty-one and I was eighteen, and I just knew this was a tragedy, but I couldn't stop them because they were "cleaning up." Letters and God knows what else besides those sketches with the D's on them—those two just pitched them into a bonfire in the yard. I was snatching out Mama's drawings as the flames were curling the white papers up, turning them brown. And they were laughing and throwing the sketches back. I suppose the "cleaners" in life do have a point in that you can sink under the weight of all this nostalgia, but that really was a tragedy. Cleaning is something that should never happen to an attic, but if you couple a house-cleaning woman to a Yankee that's just what will happen.

Now, Mama again. She also played the piano, the organ, and the violin. And she wrote fiction. A month before Daddy died she'd sold her first story to *Scribners*, and she sold five more to popular magazines before she stopped. These all dealt with Southern black life—realistic portrayals similar to the ones my mother-in-law Julia Peterkin had done ten years earlier. And they sold for about twenty-five dollars apiece, so if she'd continued perhaps she'd have made a living as a writer.

I guess, before ending, I should also say that Mama was a pretty woman—beautiful really. But beside that she had a certain pride, an assurance about who she was. She carried herself well and tried to dress accordingly, and in this last wish she had help from some wonderful friends in Philadelphia. She met these two women at the Kimbels', and they'd send her boxes of fashionable clothes that they'd been wearing themselves only a few years earlier. This did make for a strange comparison when she was out working. I remember a picture taken of her in a black suede hat with suede feather and suede suit interviewing Ben Horry, who was wearing rags with patches over patches. But I also remember a day in the Freewoods when Mama had on black lace stockings. A black woman admired them and said, "Miss Genny, I'd give anything for stockings like that to wear to church on Sunday." My mama just hiked up her dress and rolled them off her legs and handed them to the woman. And when my little brother Bill was supposed to be Davy Crockett in a third grade play, Mama took the coonskin collar off this gorgeous coat from the North and the local seamstress made him a coonskin hat. And even more of these dresses got cut down for June and me, which was also a common practice among our neighbors. I remember one really poor little girl on the playground wearing beautiful velvet dresses with lace collars. She had to go barefoot, but the family had a rich relative in the North sending dresses. By the end of the war June was working, and if she bought a sweater for herself she'd buy one for me and something for the boys, and when I got a job I followed suit. Then by the 1950s we could buy Mama's clothes too—nothing like she'd worn in the 1930s but at least suitable for her job.

June and my two youngest brothers inherited Daddy's blue eyes and blond hair. Tommy and I inherited Mama's dark hair and brown eyes. But what all five of us inherited from Mama—I should say what I hope we all inherited from Mama—was that pride I spoke of. I don't mean pride in being a Chandler, though, of course, we were. And not arrogant pride like the Flagg family were supposed to be guilty of. What I hope we inherited was Mama's pride in being what she was and what she expected each of us children to become—a brave and loving adult human being.

Daddy

THE WEDDING PORTRAIT TAKEN WHEN he was thirty-two shows my father as a large man with light-colored hair already receding far back on his forehead. His name was Thomas Mobley Chandler, and he was from over in Williamsburg County, a little place called Cedar Swamp, which is about sixty miles to the west of here. His family were from early French Huguenot stock. They arrived a couple of centuries ago, so plenty of Chandlers are around, but none that we can claim as real close kin.

He had one day of college—I guess a few minutes really. His father, a farmer with some success, had driven him in an automobile the hundred miles to Charleston and enrolled him in the military college, the Citadel. Daddy followed the railroad tracks, wore out a pair of shoes, and beat his father home. He liked farming though and stayed at it until the short war down on the Mexican border offered some excitement. From there he went almost straight off to fight in Europe with the Rainbow Division. That was one of the first divisions organized, National Guard units from a couple dozen states put together. He won a battle-field commission, up from sergeant, but this never went through because, unknown to those out on the battlefield, the Armistice had been signed two days before. And he'd been gassed in that fight two days after the war ended, and that injury weakened him for the rest of his life.

Around 1921 Daddy came down to Murrells Inlet with a couple of friends for a house party which was actually a fishing trip. You didn't have men and women's house parties back in those days. Grandpapa had built several little cabins to rent out. The cabin called Cool and Easy sat right here on the creek edge, right where my house sits today, and they rented that. Granny was probably attracted to my father first because from beginning to end she thought the world of him. Anyway, he and Mama became acquainted on this weekend, and when he got home he wrote to Mama. And she wrote back but didn't bother to mail her letter. Granny found the reply on the hall table, put on a stamp, and sent it off. They were married on Thanksgiving Day of 1922. The wedding was planned for under the graceful limbs of the big live oak in front of the Hermitage—which did happen. But a freak snowstorm blew in so they were married with the remnants of that snow still on the ground. Mama's wedding dress had short sleeves, and in the photographs she appears to shiver. She was thirty-two years old then and Daddy was too, which was considered unusually old, especially for a woman. But the war had put a hole in a lot of people's lives. We children had all these "aunts"—not kin but maiden ladies whose lovers (though I don't think they used the word *lovers* back then), whose sweethearts, had been killed in World War I. They never married, and the same was true of World War II for I had friends whose fiancées were killed overseas. And as I mentioned, Daddy was never physically strong after being gassed in that war, because mustard gas, if it didn't kill you outright, could still destroy much of your lung tissue and do all sorts of other damage.

My very earliest memory is probably of Daddy getting the caretaking job at Wachesaw and us moving there in a borrowed car. My baby brother Tommy is in a laundry basket that June and I hold on the backseat. Wachesaw was that plantation that Mama's daddy had bought when he first moved down here from Marion—a place with a high, beautiful bluff looking down on the Waccamaw River. The owner Mr. Kimbel and his wife came only occasionally. It's so strange to visit now, because once past the guarded gate they have retirement homes where my daddy's cornfield was, and that spot where I buried the Indian for Lillie, the Happy Hunting Ground, is in the service yard of a luxury restaurant.

My memories of Wachesaw are so different. Daddy put a little chicken wire fence around a section of the riverbank and cleaned up the sand so we could swim without being eaten by alligators. The fence is long gone, but the patch of sand remains and so do the alligators. Daddy kept bright green rye grass growing under that great grove of live oaks, and we had our little cottage with the porch overlooking the river. Oh, some of my most vivid memories are connected with that dark and swirling river. Me fishing with Daddy where he did the paddling and I held my little brother Tommy in the stern—though God only knows how much fishing could have been done.

Mama's brother Bubba Dick was a doctor. He was the one who had her put her hand again into the stone crab hole and was a good doctor and a good man. If some black person would get sick on Sandy Island they would send word to my father. We had no automobile. Daddy would jump on his horse and go for Dr. Dick and then paddle the doctor the four miles down to Sandy Island. They didn't have an outboard motor.

But that river was still our link with the world. When the *Comanche*—the riverboat—came from Charleston, Daddy would buy a whole stalk of bananas and hang them on the back porch. A box of grapefruit and a box of purple grapes too. The five of us would go through those pretty fast. Then no more fruit until the next boat.

Of course, if we were cut off, our neighbors were even more so. One time—and this has stuck in my mind—two of those Sandy Island men were taking a cow and a calf to the island on a homemade raft which was just some logs strapped together. Daddy had helped them load and saw them off. No sooner had the raft reached the current than the cow made a lunge and flipped the whole thing—the two men, cow, and calf—into the river. I know life jackets were around back then, but I never saw one on that river, not for us or anybody else. Daddy jumped into his paddle boat, and he saved the two men. Somehow they untied the cow from the raft and saved her but the calf was lost. And what I remember was an old woman who I will return to later, Aunt Hagar. She was the mother of one of these men. She thought her son would drown, and she screamed and came tumbling down that bank where I was standing. She thought her son was gone, but Daddy saved him.

Daddy loved to fish and to hunt. Mama called him a "Nimrod" and wrote a teasing poem that warned, "Girls, never marry a Nimrod." Actually, Daddy wrote his own poem, "Nimrods All," that went: Tommy and Corky and li'l ole Bill, / Went a-hunting down on Richmond Hill, / Tommy saw a buck! / Corky saw a doe! / Bill saw a little fawn, / And cried, "Oh no!" But Daddy took the girls out too. Once he was walking with June and me and he spotted a baby fox that had climbed up the low limb of a live oak tree. Daddy put his hat over the little fox, and we took him home for a pet—until the day Mama started to feed him and he bit her finger almost off. He'd grown up by then so we let him go.

Another time just Daddy and I were walking along the rice field bank on the far side of the river. By then no rice was growing but long dark canals still split through the rush. That one day I was trotting ahead of him, and he caught me behind the arms and lifted me straight up onto his shoulders. I was about to step on a cottonmouth, a deadly water moccasin, which he then shot.

Finally Daddy's health got so bad he couldn't run Wachesaw, and his friend and hunting and fishing buddy Ed Fulton took over. We moved to the Inlet then. I know I was less than eight, because Daddy died when I was eight. He collapsed. He collapsed on the staircase and lived on for three days. Mama's brother Dr. Dick was there, but the stroke was so severe nothing could have been done for Daddy. Still, he understood things. He couldn't speak, but he was aware. I remember slipping into his room and going up to his bed, which children weren't supposed to go near. All the adults were keeping us out so the room would be very quiet. But I slipped in, and my Daddy pulled me up on the bed beside him. He was very much aware.

He died in November of 1936, and his death affected me greatly. It was so sudden, at least to an eight-year-old. Anyway, I discovered pretty quickly that our whole world had changed. The evening after the funeral I hid behind a door and listened to an adult conversation when I was supposed to be in bed upstairs. Two of Daddy's sisters were there. Of course, this was in the middle of the Depression. Mama's youngest brother was telling her there was no way she could keep us all together. She must take us to the orphanage in Columbia. He would drive us to Columbia.

Very few times in my life do I remember my mother crying, but that evening she was crying and she said, "I don't know how I'll do it but with God's help I'm going to keep my children together." And I must say, she was the most remarkable mother who ever came down the pike. She really was. June was eleven, I was eight, Tommy was six and a half, "Corky"—who is Joe—was four, and Bill was eighteen months. Mama did have Lillie Knox to help her, and Lillie was a wonder woman. But in 1936 Daddy was gone from our lives.

Afterward Mama would often take us to the cemetery to tend his grave, and she was always talking about him, especially to the boys. They were so young they wouldn't have remembered him at all otherwise, and even for me, the rememberer in the family, there's only a sketch of this man who was so very important to all of us.

The Writer's Project

ABOUT TWO WEEKS AFTER DADDY died I stopped walking. I had severe pains in my legs, what Mama first thought were "growing pains," and she'd sit on the bed and rub my legs at night. Finally I became so ill that she took me to our family doctor, who made tests and decided I was quite anemic. So they sort of gave me a blood transfusion that did sort of ruin me. This was before doctors knew anything about negative and positive blood types. They gave me a direct transfusion. In fact, the superintendent of the schools in Myrtle Beach brought the football team to the Conway hospital to give blood. The young man they chose had positive blood and I had negative so I went into shock and they stopped the procedure, which did save my life.

By giving me that transfusion, though, they sensitized my blood to the point that—but that's another story. I had one child and couldn't have any more, and at his birth that one child, Jim, only lived by the grace of God. But that's a whole other story.

Anyway, our doctor finally decided I had rheumatic fever because I had all the symptoms, which meant I couldn't go back to school for the rest of the year. Of course, viewed from this distance, I suspect the doctor was having to guess. He loved us like his own and cared deeply, but I'm almost certain my illness was psychosomatic. Doctors weren't using that word in those days, but I'm sure that I became ill because I was afraid if I left Mama and went to school, she just might do what Daddy had done. I was determined that I was going to hang around with her. And staying out of school did work out perfectly for me. Mama had just started a job collecting folklore for Roosevelt's Writer's Project, and each day I would go with her. And what she was doing was

a very new and at the same time very old approach to history, which
means I'll have to back up.

Our Murrells Inlet is just a small section of the larger Waccamaw
Neck, a narrow sliver of land that begins at Georgetown and has the
Waccamaw River on the inside and the Atlantic Ocean on the outside.
The first attempt at a European settlement in North America was made
on its southernmost tip. Five hundred Spanish went there, but only 150
survived long enough to return to Cuba. The first truly lasting settlement
came about two hundred years later when men like Murrell started
planting rice. Eventually dozens of plantations were located along the
Neck, most extending from the fertile swamplands of the river, across
the sand hill which grew pine trees and not much else, and down to the
edge of the ocean. The Oaks, Brookgreen, Springfield, Laurel Hill, Richmond Hill, and Wachesaw were some of the closest.

We know a great deal about these planters and their visitors. The
Frenchman Lafayette landed here on his way to join the revolutionary
army, and after that war President Washington traveled these sandy ruts
of the King's Highway on his famous tour of the South. The daughter of
vice president Aaron Burr was married to South Carolina's governor
Joseph Alston and set out from the Oaks to visit her father, only to dis-
appear at sea. (They say she departed from Brookgreen, but her Oaks
plantation had a perfectly good landing of its own.) Washington Allston,
a painter referred to as the "American Titian," began life at Brookgreen.
Many of these planters were very wealthy and lived in mansions on
the Waccamaw. But during the summers they and their families fled
the deadly fevers carried by mosquitoes and stayed in cottages at the
seashore—either out on the beach or just inland on the more protected
creek front. Murrells Inlet began as one of these summer retreats, one
which was eventually cut up into narrower and narrower lots. And this
was done by men like my grandfather who came at the turn of the century to vacation and decided to stay.

And we know all of the above because detailed written records were
being kept, even by the Spanish five hundred years ago—especially the

Spanish. Back in the late 1940s Sen. Paul Quattlebaum was writing his history of our Spanish settlement, his excellent *A Land Called Chicora,* and being the head of the Conway library board and seeing my résumé showing my four years of college Spanish, he sailed into the library one morning with this great bundle of old records straight from Spain and all concerning DeAllyon's adventure in North America. He wanted me to translate them. I took them home and tried. I struggled for three days, and occasionally I recognized a noun. He was a dear old man whom I wanted to please, but finally I had to explain that five-hundred-year-old Spanish was the equivalent of Chaucer's English. I suggested the Library of Congress, and they did the job.

But the point I wandered from in discussing that damn old Spanish is that with the written record you can at least try and separate rumor from truth. Contrary to persistent rumor, the first Murrell was neither a Morrall nor a pirate. Some years back the Morrall family of Beaufort started claiming that Murrell was a misspelling of their name, and a couple of restaurants picked that up. I expect the pirate rumor is also linked to the restaurants. But the first Murrell was only a planter. He settled here in 1720, and extensive archaeological digs have been done around his house site over at Wachesaw on the Waccamaw River, and we have plats of his holdings and a record of his will. We don't know much for certain besides that.

One account claims he'd been a sea captain and that coming upon a sinking ship, he had thrown over his own cargo of either indigo or sheep (I hate to think it was sheep) to make room for the passengers of the other vessel. That's a good story, and maybe it's true. If somebody took the time they could read the records and probably find out for certain.

We know all that about the Waccamaw Neck, but that's really just the history of a small wealthy white minority. Thousands and thousands of African slaves actually did the work of diking the rice fields and planting and harvesting the crop, and in the pine lands were thousands of poorer whites that we also know practically nothing about. That was the purpose of Roosevelt's Oral History project, to somehow get a written record of how everyday people were living their lives.

And I went along with Mama. We heard all sorts of stories from both the black and the white people. These were rural people who seldom owned radios and never saw newspapers. What I mean was the oral tradition was still very, very much alive. Mama gathered stories of the supernatural and of superstitions such as the plateye and the hag and stories of talking animals like Joel Chandler Harris had collected in Georgia but with variations. And songs, all sorts of spirituals and what would be called "folk" music in the 1960s. Of course, for the blacks much of this material can be traced directly to Africa, and for the whites the material can be linked to Elizabethan England, or Scotland or Ireland two and three centuries ago, but at the age of eight I can't say I was concerned with that. I was just absorbing. And best of all, some of Mama's chief sources were already there in our lives and already telling the stories to us. When he got off work, Lillie's husband, Richard Knox, would come to walk her home. This was evening time, usually dark outside. Richard sat in the kitchen and told us wonderful animal stories—and ghost stories, very scary ghost stories. And Richard's brother, Zacky, worked for Grandpapa and was always coming by and telling a tale. And of course, there was Lillie herself bringing news from home, singing songs, and delivering accounts on everything under the sun and moon.

Often, though, Mama and I ventured out from that kitchen.

With Lillie home watching my three little brothers and my sister, June, in school, off I went with Mama to the Freewoods. We'd be driving down these sandy, deep-rutted lanes through what were called savannahs in those days—wide expanses of fields with waving broom straw and wildflowers in some and others planted all in order—little spots of green in the turned earth. And here and there were oases of cypress, limestone sinks where the dark water pooled. The cabins were scattered through this countryside, and you'd see smoke coming from the chimneys, and Mama would go there and talk to the people. Inside those homes were kept in perfect order. The floors would be scrubbed with lye, and they took such good care of what little they had.

Or other times Lucian Lance took us in his little paddleboat from the Wachesaw Landing to Sandy Island. People today will say that Sandy Island is cut off (and it's been a hard fight to keep it that way). You still have to take a boat, after all, but the Sandy Island of my childhood was much different. They had free range for hogs and cattle so every house was surrounded by a fence of wide boards—slats. The chickens were inside the fence and the rest outside. There are no cows on there today, and I haven't seen a hog, except for a wild one, in years. And the houses back then were small, rough planked—former slave cabins—just a couple of rooms with a tiny window or two and a fireplace. Those have been replaced by comfortable homes and even a couple of house trailers, though I can't imagine how they got them there. Oh, it's changed and certainly for the better, but still a visit today comes as a shock.

Also the black people on the island (and other places too) were speaking a strong Gullah. Several linguists and historians have thanked God that Mama didn't follow the Writer's Project directions. Only a couple of little books were published as a result of that effort, and in the front of one of them is a list of Gullah words to be avoided. Mama was supposed to turn everything into good old American English, but the twelve hundred or so pages she collected are pretty much as the language was spoken.

You can find much better linguistic discussions of Gullah than I could ever make. My friend Charles Joyner's *Down by the Riverside* is excellent on that subject and much else. Gullah really is a language, one that was created by the slaves from several different sources. Most of the vocabulary is English, but the basis of the grammar is African. It's very musical, and apparently the fact that Mama had a good ear and played the piano helped her in getting it down—strong rhythms and melodies, a particular cadence.

The rules for pronouns and most other parts of speech are often not the same as English. *He* or *she* can both be spoken *'e. Our* is *we*. People on the outside think it's English being spoken wrong, but actually it's a separate Creole language. Even words like using *ax* for *ask* can be traced to Elizabethan roots. Back when the Africans were introduced to the rice fields over on the Waccamaw their owners and overseers were pronouncing *ask* as *ax*.

I got so much out of that—an education and a half. I didn't really know how much until 1987 when I went into the public schools and began to speak—that's an adventure I'll return to later. Just for a small Gullah sample, ancient Aunt Hagar, when asked by Mama about the sermon given at the Heaven's Gate Mother's Day service, replied, "Me ain't no hand to fetch no text," meaning she couldn't remember it or wasn't qualified to comment. I could understand that much, but I never learned to really speak this language, and even by my time Gullah was a dying art form.

Lillie's brother-in-law, Zacky Knox, was twenty-eight when he gave Mama this account of Rabbit and Gator, and the language is mostly English. Still, the storytelling tradition it comes out of is purely African.

Rabbit and Gator

One day Buh Rabbit call Buh Gator and say, "Gator, I have so much of trouble, I don't know wedder I can make it or not!"

Buh Gator say, "Trouble! Trouble Buh Rabbit? I ain't never see trouble."

Rabbit say, "You ain't never see trouble, Buh Gator?"

"No man!"

So Buh Rabbit say, "You go on off in that broom-straw field and go to sleep and you wake up you'll see TROUBLE!"

Buh Rabbit gone on and took matches and start a blaze and took a handful of broom-straw and strung fire all round the field where Buh Gator gone to sleep at. Then Buh Rabbit let loose and gin to holler. "Trouble! Trouble! Trouble! Buh Gator, here come trouble!"

Buh Gator call back, "Where 'tis. I don't see it!" Then bout that time Buh Gator see smoke. Then he see the blaze o' fire! Flames jest a licking. And Buh Gator come a crawling, crawling-walking right on through the fire. And that why Buh Gator back crack up till today.

Lillie-in-the-Valley

FOLKLORE AND MYTH WEREN'T ALL Mama was gathering for the Writer's Project. Some mornings Mama would be in the kitchen and Lillie would say, "Miss Genny, we got to think you up another story here today." Lillie was very conscious of the fact that Mama was being paid by the number of words turned in, and Lillie's pay depended on Mama. Mama was trying to make about sixty dollars a month, thirty dollars of which would go for the car payment on the Chevrolet and twelve dollars to Lillie, which her family lived on, and the balance of eighteen dollars to feed and clothe our own family, which wasn't impossible. Mama used to say, "Any able-bodied person who lived at Murrells Inlet didn't need to go hungry." The inlet could provide enough seafood to eat, and even in the winter you could grow a patch of collards, turnips, and mustard.

Well, Lillie would often speak with Mama knowing that each word was worth money, which must have seemed a bit comical to them both since they'd been having similar "free" conversations for decades. But I'm including "Lillie-in-the-Valley" for a particular reason. Done fairly early in the project, it's a story of grief and loss. My father had died only a few months before, and I know by sharing this Lillie hoped somehow to lessen my mother's own sense of loss.

Lillie's father died around 1914 and her mother in 1918—possibly during the great influenza epidemic. The "Missus" who appears at the end is my grandmother, and the "you" Lillie refers to when she has the flu is my mother. It was at this point that Lillie brought her family to live for a while in a cabin behind the Hermitage.

I suppose you could say that Granny and Mama had rescued Lillie, but twenty years later Lillie rescued Mama. Without Lillie to tend my three baby brothers, wash the clothes, milk the cow, and cook the meals my mother couldn't have worked at all. Of course, Lillie did have a family of her own to tend. I can't claim for a moment that this situation was perfect for her—but the alternative for both our families was grim. Lillie and my mother were both finding their way. They were a team.

Also, I should say right here that I can't bring myself to use terms like "cultural diversity" and "politically correct" in a discussion. They're too "new." About half the time I can't remember to say "African American," but I'm forgiven because at my age "black" seems more natural. Actually, I can remember fifty years ago when my future mother-in-law's constant use of "black" instead of "Negro" was considered a scandal. It's hard to keep up with what's considered correct today. Some criticism does reach the point of absurdity.

Way back in the 1940s Mama gave up her fiction writing because she got a rejection from the *Saturday Evening Post* magazine saying they weren't going to publish any more pieces that showed rural blacks as illiterate and poor. Such pieces were considered demeaning. Mama never wrote another story about blacks or anything else. I suppose that was a necessary caution back then and even on into the 1970s, but I would hope that with the advances made on some fronts and with so many families of both blacks and whites now coming apart, people could look at these interviews and see the amazing way these people stuck together and the strength it took just to survive.

As for Mama herself, I've read that even before Freud came along people dealt with their emotional problems by using "the talking cure." Maybe Mama was doing just the opposite. Maybe she dealt with her mourning by listening, and not just to Lillie but to many others on Sandy Island and in the Freewoods.

Told by Lillie Knox (Age Thirty-six)

When Papa gone, I know Papa was dead before somebody come to the house. Somebody had tell me in my sleep. Let's see how old I

was. About twelve when Papa die. I join the church when I eleven
and I was working to Missus about a year before he died.

Elijah was three months old or less and that poor boy don't know
nothing about his daddy. And Mama die when he four! He wasn't old
enough to remember her features nor nothing. That night Mama was
laying down there and I been sleeping too. Must have been about two
or three in the morning. I wake up and start to cry. Mama hear me
and asked what is the matter.

I say, "Ain't nothing." But I cry. I cry. I sit up in the bed and cry
and she keep on. She say, "Tunk, (that her name for me) What you
crying for?" And just when I fixing to tell her, I hear Miss Add and
Miss Hess talking. They coming along the road. And they come on in
the yard and call Mama.

"Liz! Liz!"

"Mam!" Mama answer.

"You sleep?"

"No mam. Was asleep but wake up now! This gal here wake me
up crying. I ain't know why!"

By this time Mama have the door open.

"Liz, how you feeling?"

"Very well, Hess. How you?"

"Not feeling good."

"What the matter Hess?" And all the time Mama wondering
what they want here in the middle of the night.

"Nothing much! Nothing much!"

"Come on in!"

And they come walking in and I lie there on the bed and I cry
and I cry. I have see Daddy dead just as plain in my sleep and I know
why they come. Nobody tell me nothing but I was lying there listening. I know. I know!

Miss Add say, "Liz, where Henry?" Mama tell her, "Henry gone
in the creek. Henry full up on water-melon and gone floundering.
Take he gig and cart of fat kindling and gone about sunset to fish 'til
tide too high. This gal here say no where don't hurt her, but she keep
right on crying."

Miss Hess up and goes to walking. Walking. She goes to the bucket, takes the gourd and gets a drink and go back to walking. She hate too bad to tell Mama. Go back to walking.

"Liz," she say, "I ain't know how TRUE it is, but we come to tell you—somebody say Henry mighty sick down to the creek shore—to Buck Landing. Don't know how true he is. This just what we HEAR———."

"HENRY! MY Henry! He left here well this evening. Of course he could have took sick and die in this time———."

And I cry out: "My Papa! He ain't sick! You can't fool me! My Papa dead!" Miss Hess sound too sorry. She say, "No child. He just took bad sick."

And then I holler. I holler until the neighbors alarmed. And here comes Mr. Josiah to see what wrong. And Miss Hess and Miss Add never would say "He dead." Mama got up like she was crazy and they throw a frock on her. Miss Min had give her a round velvet hat. A round hat. Reddish. Make up with a rim. Would pull the rim down and keep your ears warm. Wore skirts and waists in that time. And she had a worsted skirt lined with brown linen. And Miss Add took a big safety pin and pinned it on. And Mama stepped in her old slides. Didn't take time for no stockings. She started bare-foot but they made her stop. She going to Henry now, going down to the creek shore, to the water.

They left me there and all the children asleep. Other children know nothing. Me the one awake. And that dream have me scared. I call Sister.

"Sister! Sister! Papa dead!" Sister half wake. She tells me, "Oh shuc! Oh shuc! You all the time imagine things."

In the meantime, Mama got to the landing. A big fire there. Driftwood bonfire. Mister Joe there and a good many more. And she stumble and her hat gone in the fire. If they hadn't been quick on the trigger she would have fallen in. That red velvet hat got burn up.

And that whole four years she lived beyond him, it was "Henry! Henry!" She all the time talk Henry. Never stopped talking Henry. We'd have good fried fish and things he loved to eat. She'd say, "Now if HENRY was just here!" and she'd stop eating and get up and leave the table. She fret so. Elijah wasn't thriving. Baby stopped growing. Measley, weasley. Grandma talk to her.

"Lizzie, that fretted milk going poison that child."

And sure enough he didn't thrive like he ought to. But back to that night, here come Mister Joe bring Papa's body home. He was on a cotton mattress stretched out in a wagon. And when they got him to the house they had to rip down a piece of the fence to the front gate. Took down a panel. Then they drive in and back the wagon up to the front door. I can hear Mr. Joe say, "Right here!" When I hear the wagon I say, "Wake up Sister! They bringing Papa home!"

She says, "Papa dead sure enough!"

"Papa dead. Of course he dead!"

"Who tell you Papa dead?"

"Ain't nobody tell me. I see him when I sleep. I KNOW. I know Papa dead."

Miss Hess had to use camphor and rub Mama and work on her. They bring the body in. Had a little cot. Must have bring that cot with them. Had to move the table and close the back door and let the cot go right across where the door opened. Big room and little bed room to side. I remember how we shut our door. Two nails, one on one side, on the other. Had to tie a string from one nail to the other. Kitchen was a separate little room off behind.

Papa was swelled until he couldn't swell no more. I remember it good as A.B.C. He swell so he couldn't get in the box. They had to draw the nails. I couldn't stay in the room and I hear through the wall, I hear them talking—talking. They was talking to Papa.

"Stretch you arm out, Henry. Stretch your arm!"

Papa have his arm drawed up, but they kept on talking like that to him and he straitened out.

Papa's mama's name was Venia. Mr. Red-whiskered Wilson what runs the mill made Mama Venia's box and Grandma Kit's box and Mama and Papa's boxes. Made them all. They carry Papa home that night. Wash him. Dress him. See after the box that day and carry the news around to everybody. Setting up at Heaven's Gate that night. Next day was the funeral. Reverend Haywood the preacher then. I remember him starting to cry. He started off: "Me and this man was like brothers. We growed up together. We tramped the Kings Highway going to the Old Ark. We hunted, fished, played and attended school together."

And then the Reverend broke down.

Papa had a sad funeral. He wasn't sick. He just died right out. I remember the Reverend asked God to help the living. He say they the one to consider. He asked God's help. Then they pass Elijah over the box. They done that so Papa wouldn't come back and carry the baby. That an old timey custom. One hold the baby on one side and pass him over the box to one on the other side.

Then for four years Mama lived at Mount Gilead.

Before she died she say, "I took sick! I going home to my Lord and my Henry!" She had pneumonia. And me, I was sixteen. My first boy was here. Paul had come. And me the only one to take charge of all that gang of children and my own boy just walking, and every one of the bunch gone down with the flu.

Friday night she got up in a chair and tell me: "Tunk (she give me that name), hand me Elijah. Bring Paul here." And she take Elijah in one arm and she asked for the pillow and she "Peep-eyed" and played with them two babies. Then she say, "I hates to leave my babies but I gots to go. Too sick. Take them now Tunk. Mama got to lay back down."

I remember how she got up and held on to the rocking chair and crept and pulled along by the chair and fell back on the bed. Mama lay down there—she looked up and sighed. "Oh, Lord," she say, "Have mercy on me. Take care of my children. Do, Good Master, for Jesus sake, Amen!"

I was sixteen. Tyler Carr come by. He been fishing in the creek. I told him to tell Miss Rina that Mama was worse. I told him to bring me some milk from Mr. Cause-er-way. I want some for Mama and Mr. Cause-er-way the nearest white neighbor and he was milking then. Cow fresh. Miss Rina come and sit with Mama and I went to work that Monday. Miss Heywood got the news and here she come. When she gone she send Miss Hess. Miss Min say, "Don't let me hear you leave you Mama, Lil."

Mama about gone Friday. She got up and gone on the back porch and pump herself a drink of water. I was down to the creek. Thought I'd get a half a dozen clams to make a little broth. She wasn't eating. When I come back inside she had been to the pump.

Mama say, "Missus going to send you all something to eat. Some milk and grocery. Try to keep these children together and be a good girl. And above all things, Tunk, have good manners to all—especially to old people. I'm going, child. I'm going to my Lord." Then she called out to Aunty Vick. She said, "Sister Vick and Brother Washie I'm going!" Those two had come from Drumhill sure enough and was to the Old Ark at Grandma house right then but NOBODY HAD TOLD HER. We didn't know they was close by until the next day.

I remember Mama slipped away at sunset the next day. I was the only one holding up. All the children in bed. And here you come. And you half fill the glass with castor oil—the pure oil. And then you finish filling the glass with milk and shake it. And I remember just as good, you tilt my head back and hold my nose and I have to breath and it gone down.

When you gone Uncle Washie asked me, "She a doctor?"

I say, "No, Sir. Her brother a doctor."

Aunty Vick come. She look around. She say, "No doctor? Ain't nobody send for no doctor nor nothing."

I say, "Auntie Vick, Mama sick, I sick, all the children sick. I done all I know to do."

She say, "Poor little Paul. The fever have him just panting. Huh! Huh! Huh! Huh!"

And after Mama put away I take all them children and move to Missus's backyard.

Genevieve Willcox (mother of Genevieve Chandler Peterkin), about five years old, as the Fairy Queen in a kindergarten play, ca. 1895.

Genevieve Willcox, at art school, Liverpool, England, December 1916

The cast of the Hiawatha Play, ca. 1912

Genevieve Willcox at the beginning of her teaching career, 1917

Thomas Mobley Chandler (on left), husband of Genevieve Willcox
Chandler and father of Genevieve Chandler Peterkin

Lillie Knox and Hagar Brown, Murrells Inlet. Photograph by Bayard Wootten.
North Carolina Collection, University of North Carolina Library at Chapel Hill.

Richard Knox, Jr. Photograph by Bayard Wootten. North Carolina Collection, University of North Carolina Library at Chapel Hill.

Vaux Hall, home of an early rice planter, Murrells Inlet. The house was badly damaged by Hurricane Hugo and later demolished.

The Garden of Eden

WHEN MY GRANDPAPA CLARK WILLCOX found Murrells Inlet he claimed he'd discovered the Garden of Eden, and he kept saying that until he died. He was born on the day the South fired on Fort Sumter and had grown up during the great poverty of Reconstruction. He dropped out of high school to help his widowed mother and worked so his five brothers could get an education, which they did—as two lawyers, a doctor, a jeweler, and a druggist. Grandpapa was a lowly drummer and went with his buggy all along the coast selling shoes. People picked from his trunk full of samples, and their size was ordered from Richmond. He came here doing that and met Mr. John Vereen, who encouraged him to bring Granny, whom he'd married in 1880, and start spending the summers.

Mama was born in 1890 and joked that she'd been conceived on this shore after one of those buggy and covered wagon trips that brought them each year from Marion. Real covered wagons and a milk cow walking behind and chickens in a cage. Lumber and tents. Coming from Marion was a two-day trip, but they had friends from his shoe selling who let the women and children sleep inside. Once at the Inlet Grandpapa would build wood floors for the tents, and they stayed in them from May through September. Mama said that they usually bathed in salt water, but artesian wells did flow in some spots. For food they lived off the creek and bought vegetables from the local gardens.

In 1906 they couldn't stand it any longer. They had a fine new home in Marion, which they left. Granny had inherited a little money, a few thousand dollars, but enough to help Grandpapa buy the Hermitage. This was the home of the Flaggs—a handsome Greek Revival cottage with four white columns and situated on the edge of the Inlet marsh. Inside had big doors and heavy moldings. Downstairs had six rooms with high ceilings and a central hall in the middle, and more bedrooms were above.

They got that wonderful cottage, and with it came a strip of land a mile wide and extending from the Waccamaw River all the way to the ocean. Grandpa's deed read that the land was bordered on the east by the Atlantic Ocean, but just to make sure, he found the last Flagg descendant and paid her an extra hundred dollars to get a personal deed from her to the beach—figuring the desolate strip of sand and scrub would at least be worth that to hunt foxes on. Well, that beach is the center of the Garden City community today, but unfortunately for our part of the family, he left all of it to his youngest son and thirteen nephews, who sold it off long ago and very, very cheaply. Grandpapa thought women had no common sense at all, no business sense. Except for beach lots to his nephews, he left seven-tenths of his estate to his surviving son and divided the rest evenly between the women—his two daughters and widowed daughter-in-law. That led to bitterness which is still felt today.

Oh, Grandpapa really was a strange little man. He decided trees shouldn't be cut except for the purpose of building a house or firewood. He just wouldn't cut timber, which was the only way he could have paid the taxes on Wachesaw. So he sold that river place and hung onto the Hermitage and the seashore. One of his money-making projects was to build the Flagg Hotel, which Mama laughingly called his one true failure. He built his hotel around 1910, and Highway 17 wasn't paved until 1934. And not only had he built too big and too soon, he hired a woman from the North Carolina mountains to be his cook. She'd never in her life seen a shrimp or a crab. I have the vaguest recollection of that woman standing in front of the lavatory and lifting one of her feet up into the basin to wash it. The hotel I don't remember at all.

After Daddy died we ended up staying with Grandpapa in the Hermitage. Granny had died, and he needed someone to make sure he took care of himself. After Grandpapa died we moved over to a humbler cottage and the Inlet kept on being the Garden of Eden.

Altogether, maybe three dozen cottages and cabins were what Murrells Inlet consisted of back then, and these were scattered along about four miles of salt marsh shore and connected up for the most part by an oyster-shell lane running along the bluff—a lane so narrow a buggy, wagon, or automobile couldn't pass, and so narrow my future husband drove off into the marsh when he was learning to drive. But in 1934 Highway 17 came along and everybody got two lanes of pavement through their backyards.

Much of the waterfront was still wilderness—whatever was wild and could stand a little salt spray. And the yards of houses both back and front were full of those same trees and bushes—moss-dripping live oaks and red berried yaupon, cedars, myrtles, and whatever else was already growing. For the domesticated plants we had chinaberry, figs and pears, and flowering shrubs like camellias, azaleas, crape myrtle, and gardenias. And St. Augustine grass grew thick and deep green especially in the shade. And of course, conchs and other seashells marked the paths and borders.

Oh, and lest I forget, many of those buildings were constructed from secondhand materials—much of it washed across from the beach during the hurricane of 1893. That scrap and cypress poles and cedar posts with a little bark left on and the stump of limbs showing. Sort of patched together, but today that's called rustic.

Beside the residences we also had a couple of boardinghouses and a couple of restaurants which were already famous for serving seafood— which Murrells Inlet is even more famous for today. We had three churches and two stores—Mr. Byrd's and Eason's—which sold everything from sweet potatoes to dress shoes, and Eason's, as I remember it, always had a flock of Rhode Island Reds escaped from their pen and pecking around the front.

Actually, there was a bit more than this, but I'll leave out the off-limit parts. Behind the stretched-out village, away from the shore was Mission Swamp and beyond that the Old King's Highway and the black communities like the Freewoods. A few black families lived closer, but most walked that mile and a half across the Mission Swamp to reach work in the houses or restaurants or creek, which was open to everybody.

Well, it's the creek and the marsh and the beach that brought people here in the first place. You don't have to actually be on the ocean—though I've always loved to walk the beach. You can stand right on the Murrells Inlet marsh shore and see most 180 degrees of horizon. I still get up for the sunrise practically every morning. And June and I sit on my porch to watch the thunderstorms roll in—to see that cast of yellow sky above the ocean and the black clouds boiling. Oh, Land, yes. We're addicted to thunderstorms. And starry nights. Or just pure blue sky. Even today, if you focus above the Garden City skyline or go down to where the actual inlet breaks into the ocean—down where the community has a new park—you're looking off all the way to Spain or Africa. That expanse is something I'm never going to take for granted. That and the creek too. June and I still kayak and swim, and the children in the family still enjoy it, which is how it should be. When we were children that creek was our paradise.

One year on my birthday Mama got me a small rowboat, very small, not more than twelve feet. Mr. Hazel Hatchel built it of cypress. Now, none of us were strong swimmers until we were at least teenagers, but we lived in the creek. Thinking back, I'm not sure how we survived. We had that rowboat, the *Zipper,* which was supposed to be the *Zephyr,* and we stayed on the water. Mama always said that nobody should go hungry with the bounty of that salt water and marshes at the front door, and we lived by that rule.

When we got out of school our school shoes became our creek shoes or else we did without shoes altogether. You can learn to do without shoes pretty quickly when you're that age. This was before those wonderful soft Keds. And those leather shoes that you'd worn all winter turned hard and stiff once you started wading in them. Horrible. On top of that our bathing suits were woolen in those days. Nothing worse than to pull on a wet wool bathing suit. Oh, my gosh, that has to be the worst experience of this life. Wet wool and full of sand. They never dried out overnight, and you couldn't afford but one. Awful, but those were our summer clothes. We'd get decked out and spend the day pulling the *Zephyr* along behind us. Of course, there was no season on oysters and clams, and you could pick them right on the banks of the main creek. We always got our oysters below the water line, but the boat traffic has ruined all that now. Most of the inlet's not polluted, but most of the oysters get rolled away by the boat wakes.

So many friends of my grandparents came for the summer that one shore-front community was called "little Marion." We children had a twenty-foot seine for shrimping and sold shrimp to these visitors. We sold crabs to one of the restaurants which back then were really selling just "fresh caught" and "local." Friends came and spent the day clamming, oystering, or picking up crabs. Everywhere you look today are crab traps, but we children just walked and waded looking for those little eyes on the stalks sticking out of their little sink hole in the mud. You'd step on the claws, grab the flippers, and lift them into your bucket. And if you got good you just scooped them up. I mentioned Mama and the stone crabs, but I never graduated to them except in one offhanded way.

When I was nine, my brother Tommy would have been six or so and my youngest brother, Bill, was just a toddler, and we somehow persuaded Zacky Knox to take us out stone crabbing with him. He worked for my Grandpapa part-time so he was always close by, and Lillie had her hands full with running the Chandler house so it was easy to slip behind her back. Tommy and I talked Zacky into taking us along, and since we were supposed to be baby-sitting Bill, he came too. No life jackets, nothing like that. We went down Main Creek 'til we were just inside the mouth of the inlet. Zacky had one paddle which he used to pole along the edge. He didn't have oars or oarlocks on that boat, and the anchor was a cement block. At the edge of the inlet mouth, at a place called Charlie's Cut, he pulled the boat up on the shore and threw out the anchor. He told us he was going stone crabbing up in a nearby drain—a small creek. He told us to sit right there in the boat. We were partway up on an oyster rock, and he made us promise to sit right there. Don't get out and even wade. Then he was gone, and he stayed gone for what seemed like a very long time.

Well, a story was circulating about a little black boy who'd had his hand down in a stone crab hole and been bitten and drowned by the rising tide when the crab wouldn't release him. Tommy and I started discussing this tale and decided that Zacky was being held down by a crab, which was why he couldn't return. We decided to go for help. We pulled in the cement block anchor, heaved the boat off, and Tommy grabbed the oar and poled us away from the bank. The tide was still falling, and lo and behold we were headed out the mouth of that inlet. The ocean waves were right in front of us.

Tommy was six, I was nine, and Bill was sitting on the backseat all of two and a half. Capt. Ira Vick was coming in from deep-sea fishing, and by the grace of God and nothing else here came his big boat. Zacky had come out of that creek. He was flailing his arms in the air and screaming at the top of his lungs. But he couldn't swim out to where we were, not that far. Captain Ira saved us that day. Three of the Chandler children would have gone out to sea.

By the grace of God and nothing else, we grew up in this Inlet. And it's still a wonderful place to be. Right in front of the Hermitage was a little dock made from spindly saplings where we could fish with cut mullet or dead shrimp—anything at all for bait—and catch two spot-tail bass at one time. Not big ones, usually fourteen or so inches. But we could fill a tub with spot-tail bass, and that doesn't happen anymore. These catches we'd share quick. No such thing as a freezer or even a refrigerator. Just an old wooden icebox on the back porch with sawdust in the bottom and a block of ice that hopefully the iceman had brought in his rickety wagon. We'd give fish away quick to the whole neighborhood, and the same with the seine shrimp. There was nothing more fun to do in Murrells Inlet than this "working" in the creek, because there was nothing else to do in Murrells Inlet. Period. Which was fine with us.

We had playmates in the summer, but not many girls my age stayed on a year-round basis. I had Maxine Oliver, the Grant girls as friends. Still, rather lonely sometimes. Children back then, at least the girls, were under strict orders about whom they played with, where they went, and what they did. Just the other day my youngest brother, Bill, said, "You remember? Ma Price had a real house of prostitution right on what is Highway 17 Business today." And he reminisced about how when he was a little boy Ma Price kept a record player sitting up in the window of her abandoned filling station. That record player would be blasting out to the whole community, and the only song he could remember was something about "I took a snort of cocaine," which at that time was a puzzle to him. That section of Murrells Inlet was off-limits to me even though I was much older. Until two ladies, retired professors from the University of South Carolina, built a house here. Miss Johnson and Miss Wheeler. They organized the community, had a branch library put in, and then ran Ma Price out of town—which, of course, the county sheriff in those days would never have done.

My brothers finally got around to inventing water skis, but that was after World War II. I'd never heard of skis, but I guess they'd seen pictures. They tacked an old pair of Keds tennis shoes onto staves from a tall barrel. Of course, once on you couldn't kick them off, and I don't know why we didn't drown ourselves. But my brothers were inventive engineers, which is why the two youngest ended up working for the space program.

Also after World War II—that first summer, I think—the manta rays came into the inlet. These are giant animals, at least twenty feet across from wing tip to wing tip and weighing a ton. We called them clam crackers, but actually that's a smaller relative. The mantas eat plankton or sift something from the sea, but they do look sinister. Black or dark gray with wings like one of those secret bombers they have now and a whiplike tail and eyes that are wide apart and stuck out from the head. They would sail out of the water and come crashing down—a great slapping sound. It seems like they were around all summer.

They'd come before, but that was the summer my brothers and the
other boys in the creek hunted them. They'd sneak up on the poor
things in the bateau and jab them in the back with gigs and pitchforks,
and after that, of course, they couldn't hold them. By the end of the
summer we would look out on the creek and there's be a pitchfork handle streaking through the water going this way, and a pitchfork handle
streaking along in the other direction. I'm pretty sure that was 1945.
We'd been through the war, and I guess things were getting back to normal—'cause that kind of behavior was normal for my brothers. But the
world was closing in or we were exploring out. Both I guess. Still, this
was our Eden and always will be.

Lillie's World

NOW THAT'S MOSTLY THE WHITE world I've just been describing. We were happy but thought of ourselves as poor and isolated, but, of course, we did have more than our black neighbors. I want you to understand not just our lives but theirs as well. Here Lillie gives Mama a general account of her life—folk remedies, a visiting preacher, and the value of a baby boy. The remedies she'd learned from Aunt Kit, her grandmother with the Indian blood. The Indians gave the black population much of their healing knowledge because, while they had the same tradition back in Africa, the plants of this new world were unknown to them. I remember Peter Carr, an old man working at Brookgreen, saying that the quinsy-light root mentioned below got so rare he finally could depend only on the Brookgreen forest for a supply. That's also known as queen's delight.

Lillie was a great storyteller, far, far better than me, and she had a great gift for getting in her teasing but justified complaints alongside her unshakable joy at just being alive. I'm certain she was sitting at our kitchen table when she told Mama this.

Lillie Knox

When you broke and got no money to go to doctor, you got to fall back on the old time remedy. I been making them chillun keep me in life-ever-lasting tea. It bitter all right—bitter as gall. But not bitter as sea sage. I make mint tea. I makes that for them chillun. Then there's wild-physic-salts. Grows just like a piece of grass—little brown roots like hair. And old-field-riglum. Pine top tea, sea sage tea, and quinsy-light root all good tea. Red root, white root, and wild-physic-salts—I depend on them. I don't trouble with no doctor.

Had a visitor to our church last night. White man from New York. Said he glad to be in this beautiful world of ours. If we enjoy it much as he do we can get a great life out of it. "Hope God will be with you all in this beautiful country," he says. Mr. E——was there too. He grow so big I took him to be one of the guests.

The Reverend preach about the chaff will be winnow away. Had a pretty good collection last night. The "world service" money is a separate money. You pay a penny a day. Of course all the member don't pay it! But it got to go in any how. Preacher be moved if collections ain't right. Preacher have to report paid up. Reverends always report that.

Medicines? Bet you'd be surprised at the medicine Mom Melia know in the woods to do her good. Ready for a plaster—no money to send to the drug store. You go out there on a country road where the wagon run over them pine roots all the time and make 'em show up. You can find them pine roots—fat, must be fat! Then chip! Chip! Chip! Put them in a pot and boil them. Skim off that stuff that come on top the pot. It looks like scum that comes up when you making jelly. Make a plaster that'll draw any sort of pain out of you. Missy goes in the bay all the time and gets white root to boil for Uncle Quinvy. Oh, Lord, they is all kind of tea in the woods. Mom Hagar all the time hunting all the debblement in the woods. That how she have all that host of grand and great-grand. Children stomach running off (used to call it diarrhea, call it colitis now), Grandma would go and get them running briar roots and carry them in the house and get some soot out the chimney and tie the soot in a cloth—a piece of soft rag— and she'd boil that briar root and soot in the rag and the little children and the big children on that for the diarrhea just a-long and a-long. And she had a little blackberry wine. And rice! She'd boil and boil and boil rice and sometimes she put a little chicken in the pot too.

Little stubby kinder myrtle, call it low-bush myrtle, and sassafras and shoe-maker, call it sumach, they makes good tea. You have the measles or chicken-pox, the old Granny woman will give you some of them hot tea and cover you down and sweat it out you.

For high fever, Grandma would rub you with camphor and quinine and lard. If she didn't have quinine, she'd give you hoar-hound
tea. And she'd keep them Palma-Christian, that the castor oil bean,
growing in her yard. You just let you fever go up and here come
Grandma with her hand full of peach tree leaf. She'd tie all them on
the back of your neck, and Palma-Christian leaf on you wrist. Fever
VERY high she'd wet collard leaf in cold water and bind them on you
wrist and collard on Palma-Christian leaf all tie on the bottom of you
feets and here she giving you hot hoar-hound tea, hot as you can
drink it and covering you down and you'll sweat it off all right. You
GOT to sweat.

Now thyme! Grandma save that for seasoning. Like she have the
preachers or any big company. She'd want to do extra—put on airs!
She'd put a little sprig of green thyme in the oyster or fish and she'd
put egg round the dish. When she have a brown baked hen, she'd put
sprigs of thyme and hard-boiled egg in all the little places on the
dish where the chicken didn't fill it. And let me tell you—children
got no business in there until all the preachers are through. And me?
I must mind the flies. She'd get a little gum stick or myrtle or yaupon
and notch it up pretty and fold a newspaper like this. (Illustrating
over broomstick.) Let me see here now. I can show you exactly how
that thing was fixed.

Grandma'd say, "Come on gal! Got to make a fly bush! Reverends are coming to dinner!"

And you can't crack! Can't open you mouth or move out your
track. Keep a steady aim. And don't make no difference how long
they sit to the table. And me so short and dumpy I have to stand on
a block to reach over their heads.

And nothing left for the children but neck. Wouldn't be no neck
go on Grandma table. They'd left the carcass and the neck in the
kitchen. All the good liver and gizzard out there in the gravy. And
Grandma going always have that company table-cloth and Sunday
dishes. Certain dishes you not allowed to use every day. Lord,
Grandma hold her head high! I got Grandma's big old iron spider

now she always bake her bread on. Aunty Vick take most of Grandma old oven to Drumhill, North Carolina. Grandma'd take that old oven and bake light-bread and cake and rolls and all right down in the fireplace. She'd bake hen and all.

Now Grandpa never did buy no meat. He'd have a bunch of hogs, piney woods rooters, and keep his good stock penned up. All the time he'd have a cow to butcher off and on. He'd kill five head of hogs at a time. And when March come in he'd hold up off on the corn and buy grits and save the little corn left to run the critters— the hog, chickens, and horse. And he'd always figure it so he'd have one hog to kill in March. He didn't go to town much to buy. But in the spring he'd go to that Midway store and buy a big old hogs-get- barrel of flour. He made his own rice. He'd plant a little bottom, a low piece of ground, back there next to the Big Bay in rice. That would always carry them. Flour was the most he'd have to buy. Grandma was so free-handed the lard would run out sometimes. She never could seem to enjoy nothing too much when her neighbors were hungry. But there was sugar and coffee. Sometimes she'd send me to the store by the post office for them. I'd go across the big savannah and come there by that dipping vat, and walk the old Socastee road down for coffee, sugar, soap, and gold-dust. Usually she make her own lye soap. But she'd buy a little store soap to wash our faces and Sunday clothes. Wash! Grandma would make you wash them clothes out in two sudsy waters and we must boil and rinse. You got to keep on rinsing until the water is clear. If the water cloudy you just march back to the pump and tote another tub of water. Pump! I pump water till my arm pure wore out. I can see Grandma right now smelling those clothes. Smelling them! She want to find out if they any soap left in them. She wouldn't allow us children to touch Miss Min clothes. No, sir! Wouldn't let us touch yinnah things. No, SIR!

"Take that woman clothes out there and dinge them," she says. "I can't trust yinnah children with Miss Min clothes!"

I so low I have to stand on a box. There the tub setting on a big old dead live-oak block. I was about seven when Grandma learn me to wash. When I home nobody there when Mama sick but me. Nobody but me to do nothing. Pick up scrounge and thing to keep the pot boiling. Corner in the kitchen pile up! I think I getting wood! Use no ax. Just rumble round the woods, find scrounge and dead stuff and broke them up with my foot. I come home totting it all tie up in a ragged sack on my head. Mama lying in bed. Mama and Papa they'd praise me up! Here I'd pitch up in the morning, start up a fire! Didn't need no kindling. Have all them little dry scrounge. Here I'd sit down on the hearth and build a little fence out of all the little limb and blow on the coals (if they been any coals) and if I have match I'd set it to the bottom and watch that little fence go to burning. Then I'd go to cooking breakfast. Aunt Jane and Mom Ella and all them old head come to see Mama. They'd look at the baby first—the new baby. I can hear Mom Ella:

"Gal. My Lord, you got a fine child!"

Mama'd say, "Shucks! This here gal come she ain't know what ahead! Just come for see! Come for see!" (She thinks the baby won't live. That how come we call Sister "Come-for-see" still today.)

But you let a BOY come, here Papa! He out front. The mens walk by Papa hail them!

"Stop by! I'll make my boy wallow you in the sand!"

The mens go look. They stand there by Mama's bed looking down.

They say, "I tell you Cogsdell, she got a bouncer all right! That's a Man! A Man!"

Papa laugh one them healthy laughs of his.

He say, "That's a man's SON! That a MAN's son!"

Poor old Papa! Old fellow didn't live to see his children get grown. Man is a funny creature. They crazy about the girl baby too. Love girl. But you just let a boy come! Take Miss Heywood to tell you about a boy! She call them "thousand dollar" child. She say Slavery time girl worth hundreds, boy sell for thousands. She say they rejoicing on a plantation when it come a boy.

Mrs. Floyd

MRS. FLOYD HAD MOVED HERE from the Appalachians in the 1920s. Her husband was a great fiddle player but that didn't pay and a bootlegger but not a successful one. One Sunday the family was at the dining room table and we heard a shot outside. Daddy said, "Somebody's been killed 'cause nobody would be hunting on a Sunday." He was right. Mr. Floyd had been killed in a liquor dispute.

But Mrs. Floyd went on being a cheerful person, and maybe life was actually easier for her then. She told Mama that she learned to write and read on her own. When she was a young girl she was taking care of an old person off in an isolated cabin and her sweetheart wrote her a letter. Her patient read her the letter over and over until she memorized it, and she took a piece of charcoal and practiced making the letters and associating them with the proper sounds. She learned to write, and all she had was that one letter.

I also remember that Mrs. Floyd and an elderly white woman had made a nice hearth rug, a hooked rug, with a remarkable cat pattern at the center. Mama admired that and asked how on earth they managed, and the older woman answered, "It weren't easy. I helt the cat down and drew around him."

Here's a verse of the "Old Gray Mare" that Mrs. Floyd gave to Mama. She said, "Now this here one was made up by the family."

> Bill come in
> And he roached back his hair!
> "There's somethin' the matter
> With the old gray mare!"

Bubba Dick

Mama's brother Bubba Dick had had a hard time during World War I and came home an alcoholic. Overseas he was a surgeon on the battle-fields, amputating limbs without anything to knock the men out with or relieve their pain in any way. This shattered him in a way. He was a very sensitive and dear man. His black patients loved him, and often just being his sister allowed Mama to get open and frank interviews she couldn't have gotten otherwise.

When we were living at Wachesaw, the plantation that Daddy was watching over for the Kimbels, our uncle often visited. When we'd lose a tooth, we wouldn't put it under the pillow. We'd wait until Bubba Dick came by. If you put the tooth under the pillow you might get a nickel or at the most a dime from the tooth fairy, but if you had that tooth when Bubba Dick came to visit, he'd go with you out in the yard. He'd say, "Let me see that tooth." Then he'd go out by the big old cherry tree and dig a small hand-size hole and say, "We're going to leave that tooth here and it's going to grow money." You could go back in a little while and dig and there's be a handful of money—quarters, whatever, all the change he had in his pocket that day. Of course, we caught on pretty quick that the money was coming out of Bubba Dick's pocket.

But my brother Bill was born right there at Wachesaw, and I must say that's another story. Bubba Dick, who was, as I mentioned, both Mama's brother and her doctor, decided it was too late to make the dirt-road drive to the Conway Hospital. June was about ten and I was seven and Tommy and Corky way below me. Bill was born early in the morning, and my aunt locked the bedroom door so we wouldn't come in the midst of birthing. We waked and couldn't get that door open, and

I guess we were frantic. I don't remember too much except that June and I crawled out the window, came in the back door, and entered the bedroom just as Aunt Pat was bathing the newborn Bill, so they did keep us out that long. Bubba Dick, who had just delivered our new brother, took June and me outside.

A big old oak had blown down—what the black people used to call a "hurricane" because it took a hurricane to blow one down. Those trees were like iron and once down would still last forever. This big old silvered trunk was lying there. Bubba Dick took June and me out to it, got down on the ground, and reached way into the hollow center of that tree and said, "This is where I pulled your little brother out."

June and I were actually quite old before we caught on that babies didn't come out of hollow trees.

Christmas

IF I SEE ANYTHING DECORATED with blue morning glories, I have to buy it. On Christmas morning we'd open our presents and then Mama would say, "Go through and pick what you want the most." We were fortunate because Mama had a number of friends who really were old maids, women who had lost the men they loved in the First World War and they hadn't married—the ones we called our aunts though they weren't blood relations. Most were college professors. They never forgot us at Christmas and sent boxes of presents and candy so we were in a position to pass on to people less fortunate, and Mama knew plenty.

One particular Christmas, Mama unwrapped a package. She didn't even take it all the way out of the box. She lifted up this beautiful white linen tablecloth hand-embroidered with blue morning glories. Mama looked and then lowered that cloth back down into the wrapping and said, "Now, I have something to give Mrs. Floyd." Well, I was nine or ten. I did not like the idea of that at all. But we drove out to Mrs. Floyd's. One of her daughters was in the yard cooking dried beans over an open fire. The husband had been dead for some time. They were so very poor.

I remember thinking that Mrs. Floyd didn't even have a dining room table to put that cloth on, and I thought Mama was very foolish. But of course she wasn't foolish at all, because she'd given Mrs. Floyd something beautiful. But ever since I've been buying whatever shows blue morning glories—pot holders, aprons, doesn't matter. I suppose years ago I should have taken a piece of white linen, embroidered some morning glories on it, and been set free of my own childish foolishness.

We, as in "we" the community, usually had a drunk Santa Claus. The Christmas tree gathering at Belin Methodist Church was really the tree for everybody because we had the only resident minister. For Christmas the church women filled little brown paper bags with an orange and an apple and some raisins—and Brazil nuts. One or two Brazil nuts because that was the big treat that you would only see at Christmas. Plus a bit of hard candy. I don't remember any gift-giving other than those little bags of goodies, and I'm certain that for many of those children this was their Christmas. And since this was white children only, I doubt most black children got even that—until the Huntingtons came and started giving gifts to them.

Santa. Our Santa Claus was a local storekeeper, and he has too many descendants here for me to call his name. He was the funniest Santa ever sent from the North Pole. He would always come to the church lit. He had a nice suit and looked like a Santa. But when he "ho, ho, hoed" down the aisle he was literally staggering. He wasn't a person who drank on any regular basis, nothing like that at all. But for some reason he had to get a little tight to do Santa Claus. And he did do a wonderful jolly job of it.

Of course, we had no electricity for tree lights so all the decorations were popcorn strings and the like. In the Christmas manger scene I always came out center stage, because if you were a little girl with long dark hair you got the honor of being the Madonna. And we children sang "Silent Night, Holy Night...'Round yon Virgin Mother and Child" with me thinking that a virgin was something you went around, like the corner of a building. That's where Mary was sitting with the child. Hard to imagine being so ignorant or so innocent.

And hearing "We Three Kings" still makes me smile. June was playing the piano, and my three little "wise men" brothers were standing up front singing "We Three Kings of Orient Are." Tommy, who was the oldest, was no doubt doing the best job while the younger Bill and Corky were dragging behind. All of a sudden Tommy just put his hand on top of both their blond heads and said, "Y'all sit down. I'll finish this myself." His brothers were holding him back.

My last Christmas story occurred when I was an adult, married and with a son. We were living upstate at Fort Motte, the Peterkins' Lang

Syne farm. On Christmas Day I was in the kitchen. I'd just taken the turkey out and delivered it to the table. A knock on the door, which I opened. A man I'd never seen before was standing there, a large man with a sad face. He said, "I don't want to intrude on Christmas Day, but I was passing on the highway and realized that this is the place Mrs. Julia Peterkin lived and because I read her books I'd just like to ride through the property. Is that all right?" And I said, "Of course it is, but this is Christmas. Are you going somewhere for dinner?" He wasn't so I invited him to Christmas dinner, and he seemed very happy to be asked. His name was Wherry, Mr. Wherry. I can't remember his first name now, though we finally did get to a first-name basis after a few years. Mama was there. Bill particularly enjoyed the conversation with him. He left about five o'clock. But we hadn't really learned much about him. He'd learned a lot about us because we did enjoy talking. We didn't hear from Mr. Wherry during that year, but the next Christmas Day as I was putting dinner on the table a knock was heard at the door, and there he was.

I've lost track of how many Christmases our mysterious guest came, but at one point my son, Jim, suggested we start getting Mr. Wherry a present, so we got him a book because Jim was of an age when he was thinking of giving as well as receiving Christmas gifts. For ten or twelve years Mr. Wherry was with us. We finally learned that he came down from North Carolina because he had a sister in a nursing home over in Lexington. Still, Jim began to suggest that Mr. Wherry was a ghost. He came and went and we didn't know anything about him. And I think Bill and I might have begun to wonder a bit ourselves. But after Thanksgiving one year we got a note from a friend of his sister in the nursing home: "Mr. Wherry's sister wants you to know that he won't be there for Christmas. He died last week."

A remarkable visitor. Mr. Wherry felt welcome enough to keep coming back, and that was his Christmas gift to us.

New Year's Eve

On New Year's Eve, Lillie's Heaven's Gate Church held a Watch Night service. That little clapboard and brick church was built around 1870, and it probably had the first black congregation to be formed here. I'm sure this service went back to that time or earlier.

About an hour before midnight Rev. Aaron Pinnacle started. With only kerosene lamps on wall brackets the church was dimly lit no matter what the occasion, but on New Year's we entered a totally dark interior—no lights at all. My first time at Watch Night service I remember being frightened by that eerie darkness. The deacons stood in the back, sang first and for a long time, and then told a story about how the cows bowed down at midnight in the stables. The cows were worshiping the baby Jesus in the manger. And the horses and all the other animals got down on their knees as well. Then spirituals were sung by the whole congregation until fifteen minutes before midnight.

Many years later I watched the balloon fall at Times Square and thought, "That's not half as dramatic as Heaven's Gate." In this still dark church Reverend Pinnacle called out from up in the pulpit, "Watchman, tell us of the night." And a deacon in the back of the church called out, "It's fifteen minutes to twelve." Somehow he and the reverend were both reading their watches, because after a while the reverend called out again, "Watchman, tell us of the night." The deacon answered, "It's fourteen minutes to midnight." That went on until the arrival of New Year's, and then the real shouting and singing began. They lit all the lamps and celebrated.

I went to more than one New Year's, but that first visit was the first time I ever saw Lillie "shout." Lil shouted. She was not very tall and was very fat. Those boards in the floor creaked with her weight. She shouted in the pew and then moved out into the aisle. Other women did too. The women shouted more than the men, though both did. Lil shouted until she fell over flat on the floor, just fell over, and some women were bending down to see about her. I guess she was really in a trance. But I thought she was dead and started crying. I was quite distraught, but Mama patted me and whispered, "It's all right, darling. Lil's just shouting. It's all right."

Lil recovered, so I recovered. And in the years since I've taken great joy in participating in black church services. Last year June and I attended a black funeral together. Seats were scarce, and they put us up in the choir right in front of the open casket. Immediately June started crying, and when it was over and we went home she told our friends, "I cried all the way through, but Sister sang every song." Well, I did. If you don't know the words you can pick them up quickly enough.

In the old days they sang without accompaniment. A person would pick up a phrase, the minister or someone out in the pews who's inspired. Incredible. Those voices. Those spirituals done a cappella. Occasionally at funerals you still hear that today. I've been to funerals at Heaven's Gate where they walk around the grave in a circle. Rosa Knox belonged to a group of churchwomen called the Rose Vine—all women. After the minister finished the burial service those women walked around the grave. One by one they'd put in a single shovelful of dirt, stand the shovel up in the pile, and continue walking. It took several hours to fill the grave. As they walked around they were singing "What are they doing in heaven today, / Pain and sorrow have all passed away. / Peace flows by like a river they say. / Oh, what are they doing in heaven today?"

We just stood there and watched until the grave was filled. Not long after, I had those four lines read at my husband's funeral. But I've jumped far ahead now.

In the start I just had Lillie singing. She sang in church and in the road. She sang in our kitchen while she was shelling peas. The famous ballad collector John Lomax loved her voice. He compared her voice to a well-known Latin American singer of that day and said Lillie could hit notes nobody else could. In his autobiography Lomax even mentioned Lillie by name and spoke of the wonderful spirituals she sang. And he singled out "Heaven Is a Beautiful Place" as one of his favorites. Mine too. Lillie would sing:

> Heaven is a beautiful place, I know, I know.
> Heaven is a beautiful place, I know.
> If you want to go to heaven and you want to go right
> You want to go to heaven all dressed in white.
> Heaven is a beautiful place, I know.

And then came many, many verses about your mama, your papa—the people who have gone before you.

Brookgreen Gardens

I THINK OF BROOKGREEN GARDENS as being the kind of place Lillie sang of—maybe not heaven but a beautiful and deeply spiritual place. Brookgreen is actually the Allstons' old Brookgreen Plantation combined with three others, and much of the classical sculpture that it's famous for is placed on the site of the Allstons' original house and garden. In that sense the property was ready-made because the tremendous oak avenue and vistas had been established in colonial times. And in addition to all that, they have almost nine thousand acres more—longleaf pine forest, all tall ancient trees with dogwoods blooming underneath and large rice fields cut from the river bottom of the Waccamaw—all this growing for centuries.

The Huntingtons arrived in 1928. My husband's grandfather Dr. Julius Mood and some friends had bought Brookgreen to use as a duck hunting club, but they couldn't afford to keep it. A Mr. Griffin bought it, and Archer and Anna Hyatt Huntington were the next purchasers after him. Archer Huntington's father was one of those nineteenth-century robber barons who'd made his fortune in railroads, but Archer was pretty much raised by his mother, who educated him by traveling. He adored Spain and became well known as a translator. He met Anna Hyatt late in life, and their marriage seemed to be very happy. She was the daughter of a Boston paleontologist and applied his knowledge of anatomy to sculpture, and her husband gave her the opportunity to excel.

The joke that Archer Huntington told on himself was that everywhere he put his big foot down a museum would spring up, which was almost true, and actually that is what I remember most about him—a very large, well-dressed, courtly man with very big feet, size fourteen at least, but then I was a very little girl when he arrived. At first the garden was to be just for Anna's work, but soon they started including others, although they did specify that the artists would be Americans or naturalized Americans. And the work was to be in the classical tradition—realistic human figures and animals.

Mr. Huntington was a wonderful philanthropist and spent a great deal locally. And he made many improvements to Brookgreen, in part, I believe, just to give people jobs. The road under the oak avenue was in a straight line, and he extended it for about four miles to end at the courtyard entrance of their ocean-side winter home, Atalaya. Designed something like a Spanish fortress (or monastery), that house has little rooms surrounding a courtyard filled with palmetto trees—and the building was done all with brick, sometimes with the mortar squeezing out the joints, the "Huntington squeeze," and everything splashed with stucco.

You can read about this elsewhere, but one odd thing that's never been printed is about the beautiful ironwork grilles that cover all the outer windows of what is really a transplanted Moorish fort. Mr. Huntington told Mama that after the kidnapping of the Lindbergh baby he was always getting threats against his wife so he had a practical reason for building a fortlike structure with bars on the windows.

Mama just lucked into the job of Brookgreen hostess. One morning at the post office a former pupil told her he'd been serving as host of the garden, which he couldn't stand. He was about to become a guard. Well, the Huntingtons were delighted to have Mama—with her art background and knowledge of local history. All she had to do was talk, which she loved to do anyway, and there weren't big crowds because the advertising was word of mouth. Mama was forty-six and stayed until she was seventy-four. And in those twenty-eight years she took one week of sick leave. A perfect hostess and so was my sister, June, who at a later date also worked at Brookgreen.

But to get back to the garden in 1938. You started with a bronze statue of the goddess of the hunt, Diana, shooting an arrow up over her head, and this in the middle of a pond that was full of local bream. Then you stepped through a gate and entered a portion of the avenue, eight giant live oaks with their limbs dipping low and moss hanging everywhere and on the ground dark green ivy. Beyond these trees was the butterfly garden, curling paths laid out over the old house foundation, and in the center of that was a gilded, draped figure of Dionysus. This god of wine sort of looks down on things and has a panther rubbing against his leg. You can see this golden statue as far back as the entrance gate, and one of my favorite stories involves this scene.

Mama was in the small statue gallery and museum to the right of Dionysus doing her job of being pleasant to people, and one day a woman came in holding the hand of a four-year-old boy. She told Mama that when they'd entered the gate and seen that tunnel of live oaks and beyond the statue of Dionysus gleaming in the sun, she had said, "Oh, this is heaven. This is heaven." And her little child had pointed to the golden figure and asked, "Mama, is that God?"

As I already mentioned, Brookgreen Gardens is capable of appearing that sublime. Its beauty can be overwhelming. But I suppose to be completely honest I should also add that I practically grew up there, got away with fishing in the reflection pools and roller skating on the sidewalks, and might be just a little bit biased.

Brookgreen is one of the largest outdoor sculpture gardens in America. More than 550 are on exhibit. Jaguars about to pounce. Wild horses thundering through the azaleas. All sorts of Greek gods and goddesses in varying degrees of undress. You see white marble carved so delicately you can hardly believe your eyes. And bronze pieces even more lifelike.

Plus first director Frank Tarbox was trained as a horticulturist, and he brought in wild plants and shrubs that grow in the borders, and they added a wildlife park featuring only the local animals because Mr. Huntington wanted a place of natural beauty featuring what was local. Camellias from plantation days grow as big as trees. The garden has incredible magnolias that date back to the Allstons' time—huge trees with creamy white petal blossoms and shiny, shiny dark green leaves.

And similar to them are the tulip trees and star magnolias. There are azaleas which in the spring defy description. They've replaced the ivy beneath the central oaks with jonquils, and as much as I love ivy, I do love a yellow jonquil too.

And poetry. Archer Huntington selected the poems himself, and they're inscribed on tablets placed along the walks. The poet Pearl Counsel Hyatt went to college with my mother, who recommended this introductory verse to Mr. Huntington. As you enter the garden you read:

Inscription for a Garden Gate

Pause friend and read before you enter here
This vine clad wall encloses holy ground.
Herein a mellowed garden dreams away the years,
Steeped in serene sweet light and muted sound.
Herein tranquility and peace abide,
For God walks here at the cool of evening tide.
Pause friend and strip from out your heart
All vanity, all bitterness, all hate.
Quench for this hour the fear of your fears.
Then treading softly, pass within this gate.
There where the ancient trees wait, hushed and dim,
May you find God and walk a while with him.

Brookgreen did seem to be a place where God would walk and you could stroll beside him. Archibald Rutledge, our old state poet laureate, is a favorite of mine, partly, I expect, because he complimented the mysticism in my own attempts at verse. I do wish I could write a poem like his "The Meeting," which is over by the Dogwood Garden.

Men made me dread to meet God,
But I found it sweet.
Ah, you have disobeyed the laws men said He made.
Yet from Him was not, "You!
You wretch for mercy sue!
You wicked sinner!"

Rather, just like a gentle father,
"Son, how your garden grows!
I love that yellow rose.
And that Parnassus seems
Come from a land of dreams.
With the fine work you've done,
I'm proud of you, dear son."

And in the same direction of that poem once stood a little statue by Brenda Putnam called *Communion,* a very old and wrinkled woman holding a chicken up to her breast. This equally old flesh-and-blood couple had come down from the upstate for the day, and Mama asked if they were enjoying themselves. The man answered, "Lady, I seen the ocean for the first time today." Mama said, "What did you think of it?" He answered, "Weren't nothing. I seen the Catawba River in flood one time." Then Mama asked the little wife which sculpture she liked best, and she said, "I liked Mrs. Noah." Mama said, "Mrs. Noah? Where did you see Mrs. Noah?" She said, "Well, she's out there holding her little chicken getting ready to put him on the ark." And this piece by Putnam was called *Communion,* a little chicken up against the shoulder of an ancient woman. I mean the visitor from the country did understand it perfectly.

Bill and I also had a favorite statue, one called *Long, Long Thoughts*—a small boy in earnest concentration. A modern boy in shorts, not a little Pan with hoofed feet. He's cupping his hands and looking down on them. He's made of bronze but sitting on a real cedar stump. People were forever putting flowers in his hands. That one's on a nationwide tour now, but it used to be set up between the golden Dionysus statue and the small sculpture gallery where Mama once worked. It was fairly new, the last twenty years or so, but *Long, Long Thoughts* is a favorite of the visitors. My husband and I met the sculptor, Charles Parks, and I said, "Mr. Parks, did you get your title from Longfellow's poem—'a boy's will is the wind's will and the thoughts of youth are long, long thoughts?'" Mr. Parks said, "Well, of course, I did, but you're the first person who ever asked me that." My husband loved that sculpture.

Now, I suppose I should include a ridiculous tale to balance out this sketch. Mr. Huntington had designed a system of irrigation that pumped water up out of the Waccamaw River and into a giant pool which was just beyond the Dionysus. From there the water overflowed into little troughs which scattered it to the plants and other pools. Now, the pump for raising the water out of the river was hidden beneath the walk that bordered the rice fields, and if it was running, you'd hear a whoosh, whoosh sound under the ground. These crazy rumors started in 1942, rumors that the whooshing sound was Mr. Huntington pumping gas for German submarines. These submarines were patrolling off our coast and sinking our ships, and supposedly the Huntingtons were somehow sending boats down the Waccamaw and into the ocean with gasoline.

Poor Mr. Huntington. Nobody could have been more loyal. He and his wife let the Army Air Corps use their house Atalaya for a station to watch the coast. They gave up their home for the war effort, but this rumor got started probably by a man who'd been fired, and I don't think the Huntingtons fired but two people—ever. But this rumor went around for years even after the war. Occasionally I'd fill in as hostess, and a man from California wanted to argue me down on the subject. He kept insisting that the Huntingtons had supplied gas to the German submarines. This was years after the war, and he'd heard it in California.

The last story has a bit of both the ridiculous and the sublime. Elizabeth Patterson, the daughter of a wealthy developer in Myrtle Beach, got interested in Indian philosophy—that of India—and in a particular spiritual leader named Meher Baba. Up north of Myrtle Beach she deeded an extensive and beautiful beachfront acreage as a center for this man's followers. (I don't think these teachings required you to abandon Christianity, because Mrs. Patterson's funeral was held in a Methodist church.)

Anyway, I believe I remember seeing Meher Baba walking along Myrtle Beach's Broadway Street wearing these sheer, flowing garments from India, and nobody like that had ever been here—nobody. And soon after that he visited Brookgreen. Mama came home from work that day just outraged. Quite a number of followers had accompanied Meher Baba to the garden. They were a large group, and Brookgreen did have these little signs stuck in the grass saying "Please stay on the walks." Well, Meher Baba stepped through the front gate and saw those ancient live oaks, and his reaction was the same as that of the mother and her four-year-old. He was overcome with the beauty of those trees with great gray-moss-covered limbs sweeping everywhere above that black-green ivy. He looked at the surroundings and fell down on his knees to pray, and all the two dozen or so people who were with him then went down on their knees on both sides, and being such a large group, they spread out onto the grass.

Immediately here came the guard, blowing his whistle and scream-ing for them to get off the grass. Mama was working over in the gallery, and the windows were open on this warm spring day. She ran to the window, and here was this scene of people trying to worship in the middle of "Get off the grass! Get off the grass!" Mama was so humili-ated, and she came home so angry that night.

Anyway, Meher Baba had taken an oath of silence long before this, and for Mama that was a problem because she did love to talk. The group finally made its way over to the gallery, and Mama was telling them about the history of the place and so forth, and something of the compassion she felt for these people and the embarrassment must have been showing in her eyes. Meher Baba approached her. He reached into his flowing garment, pulled out a single grape, held it up, and then gave it to her. She didn't know what to do so she ate it.

That's what she was supposed to do, but Mama lived a long time and died without ever knowing that. Three years ago June and I were on an Audubon birding trip, and we went over to the Meher Baba Spiritual Center that's still active north of North Myrtle Beach. These two lovely lady volunteers welcomed us. You don't have to be a fol-lower of Meher Baba, but they have his teachings there and little cabins where you can go on retreat. A beautiful piece of land. Woods thick with pines and freshwater ponds hidden behind the dunes, and all of it is kept very natural. I walked through with Ambica, one of the two women, and told her the story about Meher Baba visiting Brookgreen and the guard's actions that disturbed Mama so and how Meher Baba had given her a grape which she ate. My guide was amazed and told me that Meher Baba only gave the grapes to people who he recognized were on a spiritual level with him and that when offered the grape you were supposed to eat it.

June and I were happy to hear that and sad that Mama hadn't known. Then we headed toward the beach. We walked past these patterns of shells that Meher Baba had laid out in the sand and through dunes still thick with sea oats. We both have a habit of taking one shell from each beach we visit for a keepsake. So having arrived, I was skirting along just where the waves lapped the sand, and I spied a perfect little purple round shell. I thought. I leaned down, and the shell was a grape. I cross my heart and hope to die. Even as I was passing the spot where Meher Baba had laid out his patterns, I'd thought that this was such a serene spot the holy man's spirit could still be hovering. And that grape couldn't have been planted intentionally. They had absolutely no way of knowing that I would be coming with my story, and the event was so unusual they even wrote it up in the Center's newsletter. And yes, that grape probably had washed up from somebody's picnic way down the beach. Still, a grape is a grape. I went running back to Ambica and said, "Ambica, Ambica, I thought this was a shell and look, I picked up a grape." She said, "Eat it." And I did—sand and all.

THE JAPANESE BOMBED PEARL HARBOR in 1941, and America went to war. But that was also the year that Lillie left us and took a job in the home of a Marion dentist, a Dr. Davis. Lil's husband, Richard, opened a nightclub in Myrtle Beach and was probably making real money for the first time in his life. But one night, while defending himself from a robber, Richard accidentally killed a customer. The charge was manslaughter, and Lil needed money to "buy Richard off the chain gang." At least that's what I always heard. Mama couldn't pay Lillie more so she got her a better-paying job.

Now Lillie was living eighty miles away. She had gone out of our lives. But that first summer I went to visit my cousins in Marion. I was thirteen. I was walking on the street with the youngest of these, a girl a year younger, and I saw Lil—which was a surprise since the dentist's home was actually in another smaller community. But I knew this was Lillie. She was so stout she just rolled from side to side as she moved down the sidewalk, and I knew it was Lillie Knox. I cut loose and started running, and when we met we hugged and kissed, and my cousin crossed the street to the other side and wouldn't walk home with me. She was embarrassed that someone kin to her had hugged and kissed a Negro.

Lillie was the same as my Mama. I can't really explain how much I loved her. A few years back I was returning from the funeral of an old man I'd loved so very much, a man who'd treated us children so good when we were growing up. I pulled off the road and jotted down these lines which work just as well for my joyous Lillie.

Joy is a simple word,
too seldom spoken.
A pity.
Just a bit of it could mend hearts broken.

And last but very, very far from least is a prayer that Lillie gave Mama—Lillie said, "It just come to me after I converted."

Lillie's Prayer

Good Master, You able to hew down the mountain. You able to make the crooked way straight. You able to make a way where there no way.

Go to the Lord from the innest part of you heart, mean what you say, ax Him for forgiveness and He'll hew down the high mountain. Though you sin be dark as middle-night, He'll make them white as snow. All power in His hand. He can defend and destroy. He can make a way out of no way. He can un-block the blocked road. He'll make it clear before you eyes. He'll move all them stumbling block. Everything is in His mind.

I know my Redeemer live. I ain't know how you feel, but He's had His hand on me.

Lord, you know all thing. All thing trust in Thy hand. You can defend and You can destroy. You can lay down in one hand and pick up in another—Lord, You can make the rugged road smooth. You can make the crooked path straight. You's able to hew down the high mountain. You able to make my sins whiter than snow. Lord, I trust You for all things, for You is the God of Heaven. And You will do right. Dear Lord, I'm so weak and You is strong. Make me be the woman You desire me to be. Guide me. Guide my feet in the path of righteousness, that I may live, so when You call me by my name I'll be able to answer.

Make me be the woman You desire me to be. Guide me.

That bears repeating. That was my Lillie.

OTHER WORLDS

Cousin Sam

MY BROTHER BILL AND HIS son make duck decoys from rough brown cork, a cork which is harder and harder to find. They even tore down an old icehouse to get cork, so they were thrilled after the last storm when a World War II life raft floated up in Bill's front yard. We'd had some wind but no real high water. But here was the raft. Baffling. A bit of the canvas was still on it, but the bottom was covered with oysters, which indicated this vessel had been sitting somewhere a very long time—not floating in the ocean, but sitting. As much cleaning up of the creek as we've done, it's strange we never saw it. We have these marsh sweeps and go after trash even in canoes, but somehow this raft got past. Maybe it had been close by all those years. Anyway, the vintage was definitely World War II, and Bill salvaged this tremendous amount of cork—which is one of God's mysteries because the raft floated right into his yard, and nobody else in the world would have been excited about finding old cork—except his son, who came down from North Carolina just to see the World War II cork raft.

World War II. Mama, June, and I could do so little to help, and yet we wanted to make a difference. By the time the war started I was in early high school in Myrtle Beach, and they let us spend our study halls as lookouts in a tower on the beach. I learned all the shapes of the German planes and the Japanese planes and, of course, the American planes, and thank goodness we never saw a plane that wasn't ours. This was frightening in a way, and as the war progressed so did our concern. I can remember sitting on the bank in front of the Hermitage a year or so later looking across the inlet at the dunes on the beach and thinking one of these days German helmets are going to start rising up over those sand dunes. I mean from copies of *Life* magazine and other places you were taught to just dread the shape of those German helmets. These days when young women choose to go into the military, I just can't relate at all. I'm way behind time. Back then I was thinking thank God I was born a girl. I had these three younger brothers who were too young to fight, and I was praying the war would be over before they had to go. We were a very lucky family in that regard. I'd heard about the First World War from both my parents and knew a bit about the gruesome reality of battle.

Still, we were anxious to do our part, which we did, though that first time Mama didn't actually tell us we were doing our part. At the very beginning of the war they thought German submarines were having contact with our coastline. From Huntington Beach down to Pawleys Island and everywhere else, I suppose, they had men on horseback patrolling. Rumors went around. Some were ridiculous like the one I told about the Huntingtons pumping gas, but in another tale our side had sunk a German submarine and an American bread wrapper, a Merita wrapper, had come floating up. And then they found tickets to the Garden Theater in Charleston on a drowned German. You were always hearing about the Garden Theater. (I should say right here that I don't for one solitary minute think that Sam Byrd was in Murrells Inlet to investigate Mr. Huntington or Brookgreen or the pumping of gas to German submarines.)

Anyway, one day a man approached Mama while she was working at Brookgreen Gardens. He was dressed as a civilian but showed her identification. He was Sam Byrd from Naval Intelligence in Charleston and had come to Murrells Inlet to chart the area and take a look around and needed to fit in—no one could be wondering what the heck he was doing here. And he'd approached Mama because naval intelligence knew of her work with the army in World War I and felt she could be trusted.

Oh, Mama had a pretty good idea of the kind of cover story that would be needed in a little place like Murrells Inlet. That afternoon she brought him along following in his car and greeted us immediately with, "Children, this is your Cousin Sam." Well, we had a Cousin Sam Wolfe who we'd never met, so she didn't give a last name to our visitor and left it to us to assume this was our long-lost cousin. Then she got him a room with a neighbor. In the coming weeks he often ate his meals with us, so we children would have seen a lot of our cousin—if we hadn't already been spending practically every day with him. All day long, just about every day.

Cousin Sam had to go to the mouth of the inlet, so just about every day we'd turn this into a picnic. A picnic in those days was maybe a loaf of bread and a jar of peanut butter and some jugs of water, nothing fancy. And in those very first days we were still young enough and innocent enough not to let even the threat of Germans spoil a picnic. We'd row him out to the mouth of the inlet and spend hours on the beach. We didn't know what he was doing. Of course, since we were rowing we would go out with the falling tide and return with the rising tide, so you stayed awhile even if you didn't want to, and Sam wanted to because he was up and down the shore the whole time.

Finally Sam finished his mission and returned to Charleston, but several years later when I was grown up, sixteen or so, he came back, and lo and behold he was in a lieutenant commander's uniform. He'd just returned from the European theater and came to tell us good-bye before he went to the Pacific. That's when we learned his true identity. Before the war he'd been a Broadway actor starring in *Tobacco Road,* and he'd already published a novel called *Small Town South*. I guess acting the spy came natural to him.

Now, some years later my future mother-in-law would say I shouldn't marry her son because he was so much older and somebody my own age would come along. But actually I'd already been proposed to by a much older man. When he left the Inlet for the first time, my cousin Sam said, "Sister, will you wait for me til you grow up?" or some such. Then when he was going to the Pacific we were all out in the yard saying good-bye, the whole family, and he said, "Sister, what do you want me to bring you from the Pacific?" And I can't believe I said this, but I answered, "Oh, nothing. Just kill one Jap for me." But that's how we felt. We'd ride the school bus singing "Praise the Lord and Pass the Ammunition and We'll all go free. Let's all remember Pearl Harbor as we did the Alamo." We were just so indoctrinated. I'd been dreading the shape of German helmets for some time now and seeing the Japanese as terrible slant-eyed cartoon characters. And the truly horrible thing about that story is that Sam went out in the Pacific, and he sent me a photograph. He'd been a hero in the D-Day invasion in Europe. He'd held some part of the beach that wasn't even supposed to be landed on and been written up in a Yank magazine. But I don't think he was actually in combat in the Pacific. By then he was doing public relations. Still, from there he sent me a photograph of himself standing over this dead body on the beach and pointing a pistol at it. Written on the bottom was: "This is the one I killed for you!" All of this is hard to imagine. Even then it was hard to imagine.

I finally put that photograph in the fireplace and burned it and tried to forget I'd ever said "Kill one Jap for me" or could have even thought such. But it's incredible he would send me that photograph in the first place.

We civilians had such strong feelings during that war. We had them again in the Korean War but no anger like that against the enemy during Vietnam. When I worked as a librarian in Germany during the early 1950s I had a German secretary who told me they'd been so indoctrinated by Hitler that they believed every word they heard. And if he was speaking that night she'd go and hear him still. She said, "You Americans weren't that indoctrinated," and she was right.

The Crash Boat Crew

In the second year of the war the Army Air Corps came to Murrells Inlet and set up a crash boat operation. In exchange for one dollar Grandpapa leased them a spot of deep water for the duration, and they built a tremendous wharf, the biggest and heaviest-timbered anybody around here had ever seen. All of these beaches that are so crowded today with vacation homes and high-rises were empty back then, so the military had a clear field, and they put targets as big as the side of a house running right up to Murrells Inlet and what is now Garden City and Surfside. Big canvas targets stuck way up in the dunes. Surfside people working on their gardens will still occasionally find a caisson shell, and we still find them in the Inlet too. That shell is about two feet long. And those smaller fifty-calibers, they'd go zzzt, zzzt, like that, when they hit the water— like in the movies. From our front yard we could watch them striking.

Most of the planes were coming from Shaw Field up at Sumter, and several of the pilots told us that they would begin their run over the fields of the Freewoods, and since our home, the Hermitage, had bright asbestos shingles, that gave them a broad white sight to line up on. Well, we knew they came right over the house because we had a lot of broken windowpanes. The concussion would rattle the windows and the china on every shelf. They'd open fire as they came over.

But we weren't the only ones affected. Some men were playing poker over at Curlew Point, and one of those seventy-five-millimeter shells came right through the roof and shot the chandelier out of the ceiling right over their heads. And my future mother-in-law's house, which was only two doors away, had a shell go through my future husband's bedroom which came out on the front porch. She wasn't using the house at the time, but she went up to Shaw Field to discuss this, and they said if they got any more complaints from Murrells Inlet they'd close the entire village for the duration. So she shut her mouth.

But despite all this our direct contact with the servicemen became very close and very friendly. The crash boat crew that was stationed at the air corps giant wharf was made up of men who had been fighting overseas and who had come back. It was considered an easy duty, a way of decompressing, of recovering, for there was no work to speak of. They just kept up the boats and would go in a hurry if a plane crashed. The one horrible part was that they never recovered a live person, only pieces of bodies. I remember us children watching them come up to the dock with those white bags. We knew what was in them.

My sister, June, is three years older than I, and she married one of the crash boat crew, Ken Hora. He was from Buffalo, New York, but came here by way of combat in Italy. I guess eight or nine local women married those men. I was just young enough not to be dating, but they were my good friends—not boyfriends, just friends. You see, because Mama had worked with the Rainbow Division during the first war, she understood their homesickness, and working in Germany a few years later I'd come to understand as well. Mama literally threw open our home to that crew and ran a service club without it being called that. We had horseshoes in the yard, and they'd play horseshoes with my little brothers and each other. We talked to them about lots of things, about the creek and about our lives.

One Christmas those young men showed up and had a big fire roaring in the fireplace when we came downstairs. We weren't the only family treating them this way, or to be treated this way. The Olivers, who had the restaurant Oliver's Lodge, did the same and so did others.

Every Sunday an army chaplain held services for the crew, and many of us attended that as well as our own church. What else could you do? Growing up we went to Sunday school and church at the Methodist church and then met our Presbyterian friends for their four o'clock meeting. Grandpapa was that strict about Sundays. On the Sabbath we couldn't even swim, so it seemed quite natural to go and pray with the chaplain too. And I'll never forget one Mother's Day Sunday the men of the boat company (which is what we officially called the crash boat crew) presented my mother with a beautiful armful of roses because she'd been most like a mother to them. But there were other "mothers." In a community as small as ours everyone knew these twenty or so men.

They let us go in the crash boats with them. Large boats, long bowed speed boats and cabin boats larger than anything we'd ever seen and faster, and we'd be out there riding in the ocean leaping over the waves at forty miles an hour. And my brothers would go down to the dock at night, and they taught the soldiers how to gig winter trout when the water got ice cold. My brothers had trained a porpoise—a plain out-in-the-wilds porpoise. They named him "Old Joe," and he'd come up the main creek when they called, driving all those winter trout ahead of him. The men would stand on the bank and gig all the fish they wanted, which was a special treat if you'd grown up someplace where the porpoises weren't trained—like upstate New York or Iowa. And my brothers would eat a lot of their meals in the crash boat mess hall because sugar was rationed but they had an unlimited supply for pies and the like.

All those are happy memories, but there's one particularly bad one I'll never get rid of. I was sitting on the creek bank in front of the Hermitage 'cause a lot of times we'd just watch the planes practicing. When they were firing in formation they'd come in threes and circle first, then break formation and fire. When their ammo was gone they'd return to formation and go home. These were A-26's and B-25's, long gray fountain-pen shapes, except with wings and bubble-glass protrusions and huge propellers chopping the air. One afternoon three of these were circling to reform, and as they did the wing of one knocked the tail off another which started spiraling down. This was horrible to watch, especially because the tail gunner had escaped and opened his parachute. But the parachute caught in the pieces of the tail, so he fell as well. All that flapping white silk got snatched out of the blue sky, and the tail gunner went straight down and head first.

Before the plane hit the marsh I was screaming for Mama, who happened to be home. She drove me fast to the boat company, and I jumped out of the car and ran into the main building, which was the mess hall and headquarters combined. A colonel was there from off doing some kind of orientation. Somebody was always posted as lookout on the wharf, but today they were all inside because of this meeting. I came through that screen door. I knew those men so well but I'd never been inside. Little boys could go in there but not girls. I burst through that door, and this colonel yelled out, "Since when are women allowed in this building?" I was fourteen, and he scared me to death. I just started crying. Then I saw the cook Slim. I saw his face and focused on him. I said, "Slim, a plane's gone down." And they all jumped up and were gone from the dock in less than a minute.

The plane had fallen in the marsh and was burning. When they got there the two boys in front were trying to break the glass of the canopy and get out. The tail gunner with the parachute had died from the fall, but those two were still alive. But because of the boggy mud and the marsh the crash boat crew couldn't reach them in time. Both died.

As I said, that's a horrible memory, but toward the end of the war I came close to getting killed myself. I was a freshman in college, and I brought a friend home for the weekend. They'd put an announcement in the newspaper. No more practice firing on Sundays! It had been seven days a week until then, so now we had a day to go fishing or go for a picnic, which is what I decided to do with my friend. We rowed out to the beach, and since the targets were the only shady spots we took our little basket and headed up behind one of them to eat. We settled down on our blanket and spread out sandwiches and poured lemonade and gazed around thinking we were the two most fortunate humans of our acquaintance. Then we heard an airplane and looked out from behind the target.

All that saved us was that by this time the planes were circling the targets once before firing and the pilot saw us. We grabbed up the pieces of that picnic and ran like bats out of hell. But, of course, that wasn't enough. They still kept running the announcement about no practice firing on Sunday, so my sister, June, and I took the wife of the Myrtle Beach provost marshal out fishing. We figured this was safe because we were off from the beach which was officially safe anyway. But no sooner did we anchor than here came the planes. Up came the anchor, line twisting everywhere and the oar jumping out of the oarlocks like they were alive. That time the bullets went zzzt zzzt in the water, but instead of our viewing them from the distant front lawn they were hitting right beside that tiny boat—in fact on both sides of that tiny boat. Those were two bad experiences. And in that last one my sister, June, even jumped overboard as if that would have been some kind of protection.

But June married Ken, so there is a happy ending here. In my childhood the Yankee-Southern antagonism was still pretty strong—what they today call an "attitude." And World War II did so much to eliminate that in the South. One of the men in the boat company—one from Ohio—was thumbing a ride trying to get from the Inlet to the Myrtle Beach air base. Practically no traffic on the roads in those days, but finally an old rattletrap car, some kind of hand-cranked Ford or Chevrolet, came along. He had his thumb out. He was in his uniform, of course. The car stopped. An old-timer was in there by himself. He rolled down the window and called out, "Young man, where you from?" And the young soldier from the boat crew answered, "Ohio, sir." And from inside the car, "Well, you can walk through the South like your grandpappy did with Sherman." Then he drove off and left the young man standing there.

So that was the attitude here in the South, and I must admit that even my Mama and I felt a variation of that—the suspicious variation. Here was this very handsome and very nice man from Buffalo, New York, Ken Hora. He had a year of college before the war and wanted to study medicine in the future. He was a tail gunner on a plane in Italy, and now he was in on the boat crew. I'd just gone off to college for my freshman year, and June was working as a secretary for the provost marshal in Myrtle Beach. One day she came home from work, and this new

young soldier was playing horseshoes with our brothers. They introduced him: "This is Ken Hora."

Darn if June didn't write me a letter that night saying she had met
the man she was going to marry. Well, I almost fainted when I read that.
She was just twenty years old, and she'd known him all of three hours.

At my college you weren't allowed home until Thanksgiving, but I
took the letter straight to my dean and said I had to meet this man. I
was really disturbed and she let me go, and I did like Ken. We all liked
him very much.

But as much as Mama was taken with Ken, she was disturbed by
this prospect of marriage—since the proposal itself had come pretty
quickly after the written wish. No matter what, Mama knew nothing
about him except what he said about himself. His grandparents had
come over from Germany, and goodness alive we didn't know anybody
with that sort of background in Murrells Inlet or even Myrtle Beach.
But suddenly Mama's reservations were gone and she was delighted
with the match. Many years later I discovered the reason why. Somehow in conversation she'd learned Ken was a Lutheran and somehow
picked up the name of his church at home. She wrote a letter to his
Lutheran minister and got an answer back saying that she was a fortunate woman indeed if her daughter was lucky enough to marry Ken-
neth Hora. And we all did laugh about it when that letter turned
up—and as I said earlier at least eight others on that boat crew married
local girls. The marriage of these Northern men to Southern women
did help to put the Civil War to rest, at least in our little neighborhood.

So that was World War II at Murrells Inlet. We had blackout curtains
on the windows and planes firing on the targets, so we felt very close
to the war. With all those airmen being killed practically in our front
yard we got superstitious, and the boat company boys helped us along
because they were superstitious too, for superstition does thrive on
uncertainty. We all began to notice if one airplane crashed, within two
weeks two more would. If you had one, soon you had two more, and the
saddest part was that nobody survived the crashes. Not one man lived.

Also, during the evening ships would be burning offshore and we'd know that something had been torpedoed. The shipping lanes weren't that far away, and many tankers were moving up and down the coast. The Germans would sink those, but sometimes we would sink the German submarines. I can remember Mama on the porch of the Hermitage—us watching those big red glows out on the ocean. Mama would say, "Oh, we don't know if they're German boys or our boys, but somebody's sons are dying out there, somebody's fathers are dying out there." We really did have a feeling that the war was going on. We were very conscious of the sacrifices being made. That's the way it was. I guess that's what war is all about—somebody dying out there.

People Mama Brought Home

UNTIL 1934 WHEN HIGHWAY 17 finally got paved, Murrells Inlet was isolated. You didn't drive a dirt road to Myrtle Beach every day, and it was dirt to Conway and dirt to Georgetown plus in that direction you took a ferry. No television. And the radio didn't give all that much of a picture. Even after that road was paved we were pretty closed off just like most of the South. But World War I had at least made Southerners aware that other worlds existed or at least another side of the ocean existed, and in school we were being nudged along. I took geography a year after Daddy died. That was the fourth grade, and we studied the Eskimos. Well, I was so cold-natured as a child, and good Lord, we were living in the drafty old Hermitage with only fireplaces for heating. At night Mama had squares of an old wool blanket, squares the size of baby blankets. Each child warmed his square in front of the open fire, bundled it, ran, jumped into bed, and wrapped his or her feet up. Otherwise you couldn't stand to go down into those icy sheets.

So in geography we were studying about Eskimos in Alaska and how they lived in ice houses and got on their hands and knees in the snow to crawl inside. And they ate blubber, and I never did like fat meat, and they wore clothes made out of animal skins—all of which sounded like the most wretched existence on earth. And then, I suppose, to save her sanity Mama began to read the encyclopedias at night. Daddy was gone, so she read these books, and at the dinner table she'd tell us what she had read. Unfortunately Alaska begins with an *A* and she'd started with the *A* encyclopedia. She would say, "Children, when I can save enough money I'm going to move us all to Alaska. They say that strawberries grow as big as teacups and the cabbages are as big as dishpans. When I can save enough money, I'm going to move us to Alaska."

I couldn't stand that. I would pray, "Please God, keep us poor. Don't make us move to Alaska." And my prayers were answered. We stayed broke and didn't go, so in her old age Mama would say, "Well, I never got there and I won't get there now, but I'm going to fly over on my way to heaven." My sister, June, and I did go there summer before last, and that trip really had a sentimental feel. Plus, we went in August, which is the worst month to be in Murrells Inlet and the best to be up there. And plus, we stayed in a wilderness lodge on top of a mountain. Heavenly.

But I'm telling you this so you'll understand that while Mama couldn't send her children out into the world, she could bring the world to them and not just through reading. The people from off that she brought home would fill a book of its own. Once she returned from Brookgreen Gardens with a very old man and his wife and a little boy. This was Father Adams, a retired Episcopal priest, and his wife Mrs. Adams, and their grandson Seth Worthington. The family group had driven as far as Brookgreen and then run out of money for gas. They were headed for Florida but instead spent the winter with us. Gradually Mama picked up the facts that Seth's parents were separated and that the grandparents hadn't exactly kidnapped the child but had taken him and nobody was supposed to know where they were. Something weird.

Anyway, lo and behold, here they were. Grandpapa had died not long before, so the old couple got his bedroom, which was the biggest in the house, and Seth, being their age, slept with my brothers and attended school with them. Actually, when my brothers grew up, they confessed that they didn't like Seth all that much because he was from Connecticut and well-mannered and because he wore nice little corduroy knickers.

I don't really know how Mama managed this financially, for she was already stretched pretty thin. But I think she wanted a man around the house, so in that sense she was getting her money's worth. Father Adams

took it upon himself to be our religious instructor, and usually we little Methodists had to have an Episcopal morning and evening prayer
session. Catching that school bus in the almost dark was hard enough,
but now we had to fit in morning prayer. And no matter how much
homework we had, evening prayer was prayed before going to bed.

Somehow the rector of the Georgetown church finally learned
what Mama had done and made some arrangement with the church in
Connecticut so Father Adams's retirement check was forwarded, and in
the spring they moved on to Florida.

Another time (and this was during the war) a navy chaplain's wife
with two small children showed up at Brookgreen in a similar predica-
ment. She had run out of money trying to get to Florida, and her husband was overseas. Mama brought her home, and those three stayed
most of that summer. And one thing that woman did appalled Mama.
The Red Cross finally made a connection with the husband and finally
money was sent, so she packed her car and went. But she left behind a
little metal rack that drained dishes in the sink. Mama didn't have one
and was glad to have that memento, but the woman wrote from Florida
asking her to mail it. Mama couldn't believe what she was reading, and
I don't think she ever sent it.

We might as well have been running a bed-and-breakfast—except
the lodging was free. Dr. Morton—now, that was a case. Dr. Morton
was a medical doctor. I don't know how she got to Brookgreen, just got
off the bus I suppose. She was quite elderly and dressed all in black. I
believe she was one of the earliest women doctors. By then we'd moved
into a little house close to the Hermitage. I gave Dr. Morton my room
because it fronted on the creek and was the nicest. But the only tub was
in that bathroom, so I slipped in there one morning while she slept, and
a dagger knife was on the bedside table. I thought, "This is a woman surgeon who would know how to use it." But I know she must have carried it for protection and maybe been afraid of us. Somehow or
another, somewhere along the line, she climbed on a bus and went on
to Lord knows where.

I was home from Germany and getting ready to marry Bill when Dr. Morton came and went, so this taking in of guests had gone on for many years. Oh, I'm not complaining. These people were an education in themselves, and the next one I'm mentioning was one of the best. John Lomax was the curator of folk music at the Library of Congress, and he and his son Alan together collected ten thousand songs. He met Mama when she was working on the Writer's Project and in the late 1930s visited several times. I remember going to Heaven's Gate Church while he was recording black spirituals. The church had no spare table, so he'd raised the window and set his machine on the sill. The record got cut right there. The little needle went around and a black thread peeled off as the people were singing. All these records are in the Library of Congress somewhere.

Mr. Lomax's wife sometimes came with him. (She'd been Miss Terrill before they married, so he called her "Miss Terror.") And for a treat Mama took us up to Floral Beach, which is Surfside Beach today. Unless we were going straight across the inlet in a boat this was the closest ocean to us, and though it's hard to believe, that ten-mile drive was an all-day adventure. We had jugs of water and lunch with us. In the month of June we went to walk the beach and watch the sea turtles lay their eggs at night. Then we'd come back in August to lie on the beach and watch the shooting stars at night. Mama would tell us the constellations and what was happening up there—both the *Bulfinch's Mythology* version and the astronomers' version. Mr. Lomax and his wife went on one of those August trips, and he sat by the fire singing "Come along little dogies, its your misfortune and none of your own. Come a ki, yi, yippi, yippi, yi." He was from Texas and had started out as a collector of cowboy songs before branching out into the rest of the South. He was the first to record and popularize "Home, Home on the Range" and many others. That was early in this century. He collected the old mountain music and loved Mrs. Floyd. He'd gone into prisons and black churches—anywhere. He became friends with the singer Leadbelly, whom he met in a prison and who went on to have a distinguished career. I'm told John Lomax was considered a troublemaker in a lot of places, but he was welcomed around Murrells Inlet. He made many of his recordings right on the porch of the Hermitage, and the recordings say this.

As far as I know, John Lomax's only true sin was to break Mama's chair. She'd lost most of her things in the Wachesaw fire but now had her great grandmother's rope-leg Sheraton table and ten fiddle-back chairs. You couldn't have called Mr. Lomax refined, not by a long shot. He claimed to have come from "the upper crust of po' white trash"— a family who had left the absolute poverty of Mississippi for the less absolute poverty of Texas. One night after dinner, we five children still at the table and all, he lit this big cigar and leaned back in his fiddle-back chair. The legs popped out, and the chair broke into four pieces. Mr. Lomax just got up, pushed the wreckage aside, and sat in the one next to it. Never said a word about the broken chair. I mean, he really was a cowboy, just so different from any man we'd met. And they stayed with us three or four times.

Actually he went with us to Floral Beach twice. June was the month for sea turtles, August was for shooting stars, but September was the mullet running. Sabe Rutledge, a black man, ran an independent fishery there. Sabe and his men had a lookout, something like a lifeguard tower except higher, and the man up there would look for dark shadows on the ocean which were the schools of mullet. Then the crew would jump in the rowboat with a net and row out and surround the fish and pull the net in. Well, those men would always have sweet potatoes roasting in a fire on the beach, and they'd fry the fresh-caught mullet and you'd eat right on the beach. You don't ever have food like that again, not in any restaurant in this world. Mr. Lomax joined us on one of those September outings and had a grand time. But glancing back at the above description, I realize Mama's company was what we children valued most and what the Lomaxes had come for as well.

Still, knowing John Lomax had its value. When I was a freshman at Coker College, John Lomax was the guest speaker of our "Literary

Festival." This was 1945 and I hadn't seen him in years, not since I was a child. I guess I bragged to my English teacher that I was acquainted. So suddenly I was to introduce the famous ballad collector when he spoke, which scared me to death because this was a statewide program. Fortunately, I had dinner with Mr. Lomax and his wife at the home of one of the founders, Mrs. Mae Coker, which did relax me. And then when I stood up on that stage and introduced him, John Lomax got up out of his chair, kissed me on both cheeks, and announced, "Now, that was worth coming all the way from Texas for." Of such memories should the world be built. I tell you, I had it made with the student body for quite a while. What a dear and interesting man.

The photographers—I shouldn't forget them. Doris Ullman came to the coast, and she and my future mother-in-law collaborated on the photography collection *Roll, Jordan, Roll,* which is considered a classic. But actually we had the most to do with Bayard Wootten, who was equally talented but isn't as well known. She had a young man driving her and used one of those old-time cameras with the tripod and cloak over your head. And of course, when she and Mama went I went along. Years and years later Charles Joyner and my mother started searching for those photographs. Mrs. Wootten's studio in Chapel Hill, North Carolina, had long been closed. They checked the Library of Congress and then the University of North Carolina. No luck. Then recently a friend mentioned that UNC had just been given a new collection of negatives. I called, and lo and behold they were Mrs. Wootten's. Kincaid Mills and I had been working on a complete edition of Mama's collection of folklore and songs, and we went straight there.

The librarian had no idea who was shown in these negatives. We looked at them on a light screen where everything is backwards and these black people had white faces. This black world and this white world I'd been used to all my life were completely reversed, totally backwards, and neither my mind nor my eye was oriented. Then suddenly I saw this white face with this smile. I said, "That's little Richard Knox!" Richard was Lillie's son and just a year older than me.

I started crying right then, because I knew I was going to be able to recognize some faces. I asked the librarian to back up and let me start over. I realized I had to look for live oak trees and rivers and savannahs. Mrs. Wootten had photographed all over the South, but I was able to recognize the landscapes of my childhood. Then all in reverse, white instead of black, there was Aunt Hagar. And there was Lillie Knox. I was just crying. The librarian had tears in his eyes too. He said, "I wouldn't have believed there was a person on earth who could have given a name to a single one of those people." I couldn't believe it either. I'd found them after all those years.

The Hermitage, ca. 1910

United States Post Office,
Murrells Inlet, in the 1930s

Ken and June Hora on the Government Pier, Murrells Inlet.
In the background are Tommy Chandler and John Herpel.

Genevieve Willcox Chandler at Brookgreen Gardens, 1949

United States Army Air Corps crash boat operating from Murrells Inlet during World War II

Genevieve Chandler at Radio City Service Library, Bremerhaven, Germany, 1952

Genevieve Chandler, Library Story Hour, Bermerhaven, Germany, 1951

Genevieve Chandler at United States Army Service Club, Bremerhaven, Germany, 1952

The Gray Man

CAPT. BILL OLIVER TOLD ME about seeing the Gray Man. I never saw him myself. In 1893 Captain Oliver was working for the Lachicotte family. He had to have been a young man then. He and Miss Emma married probably around 1895 or 1896. And then those two ran Oliver's Lodge for many years as a boardinghouse—one known for good cooking. But let me back up or jump forward, as the case may be.

In 1989 Hurricane Hugo struck along here, and then the following year my stepgranddaughter was living with me. This was during her time in high school and college. Her mother had died, so she was with me. She'd try to get me to watch this television show *Unsolved Mysteries* with her, but I never would. So one day I answered the telephone. The voice said, "Mrs. Peterkin, I'm Matt Klineman, the producer of *Unsolved Mysteries,* and we want you to be on our program and talk to us about ghosts." I said, "No. I really can't do that." He said, "Well, we could disguise your voice and put you in shadow so nobody would know it was you." I said, "Well, if I was going to do it, I'd just do it. Certainly not like that." He went on to say that the Georgetown Chamber of Commerce had given him my name and that my appearance on television would give our locale national coverage that the tourist industry needed. But I still wasn't going to appear in front of millions of people and talk about how Alice Flagg haunted the house I grew up in.

He told me he'd call back, and he did several times without success, and then he did a smart thing. He sent a very attractive young man to talk to me, and he was just so nice I gave in—at least partway. I persuaded the producer that if he carried out his plan of covering all the ghosts along the coast of South Carolina, he'd just have a glimpse of this and that. Instead he should concentrate only on the Gray Man and tie the program into Hurricane Hugo, since several people had seen the Gray Man before that recent storm. I would repeat the story Capt. Bill Oliver had told me when I was growing up and leave out me seeing ghosts and all that foolishness. Now back to the Olivers.

Maxine Oliver was just a little younger than I am. I'd be playing with her at the Lodge, and Captain Bill was often telling us stories. He was a stout old man with wrinkles around the eyes from seeing so many sunrises, and he sat in a rocker on the porch. This is what he said about the Gray Man: "I was working for the Lachicottes and Mrs. Lachicotte said, 'Captain, we've had this northeaster blowing and we're going to have a storm. You'd better go over to the island.' At that time there was no real causeway to Pawleys. Just a little shell bank that had been laid through the marsh. You could cross but not at a full high tide. In the winter months we were keeping the cows in pasture on the island because you didn't have to worry about them getting off." Not to interfere with Captain Bill's story, but they were still keeping cows like that when I was a girl. Cows that would wander into the marsh and get stuck in the mud. I can remember hearing those cows bellowing at night when the water was coming up to drown them. Anyway, that was the situation. The cows had to be moved to high land. Captain Bill's account went on like this:

> I left the house and went over to the island. I walked down to the south end where the cows were. I had a stick in my hand. I got behind the cows and was herding them through this little tunnel of trees. They were ambling along in front and just occasionally I'd have to tap one to keep them moving. So there I was coming along and there was an old man standing over in the bushes, just off the path. He looked like to me he'd just climbed up out of the ocean, he was so wet. It wasn't raining hard. Just a little misty rain had started up but not a bad rain. But he was soaking wet. And he had on strange clothes. He had on a funny little cap like what we used to call a cooter shell cap, one with a rounded brim. He had on this funny hat and a double-breasted coat with brass buttons. I thought he looked like

some sort of old sailor, but the fact was, I'd never seen him before. I thought he better get off the island if Mrs. Lachicotte thought I ought to bring the cows off. So I hollered at him.

The wind was blowing but I hollered. "Hey, mister, you better follow me off the island. We going to have a storm here tonight." But he just stared at me. I thought maybe he didn't hear me so I moved a little closer and I said, "Hey, mister, you better follow me off this island. We going to have a storm tonight." He just stared at me and didn't say anything. So I just said, "You old fool, stay here if you want to." I walked on home and got the cows put up in the barn. I went in to tell Mrs. Lachicotte I'd shut them up in the barn secure. I also said, "You know there's an old man over there on the island. I never saw him before in my life but somebody ought to go make him come off. I hollered at him and told him a storm was coming and the tide's going to rise and he can't come off that causeway." She says, "What'd he look like? What'd he look like?" I told her what he looked like and she said, "Captain, you saw the Gray Man. We surely are going to have a storm." And that was the Flagg Storm, the great hurricane of 1893.

That's the story as I heard it from Captain Bill when he was an old man. But, of course, people have been seeing the Gray Man before a hurricane ever since. And invariably, if you are lucky enough to see him, your house is spared by the storm. Now, who he is exactly—there are a number of stories concerning that. He could have been old Mr. Percival Pawley, for whom the island was named. But the story they used on *Unsolved Mysteries* was of a young man who had been very much in love with a young woman. This was happening well before the Civil War. There's been a storm while he was traveling, and she thought he'd been lost at sea. So she married someone else, but he came back. He finished his tour of Europe and returned to his family who were summering on Pawleys Island. And his first thought was to see this young woman with whom he was in love, who was also on the island. He jumped on his horse and his servant was behind him, and they went riding down the beach through the marsh toward her home. He hit a bog of quicksand, and as his horse sank in he was thrown headfirst and killed. So he never got to see his girlfriend who was married to someone else. She had a dream shortly after his death that a very bad storm was coming and they must leave the island. But the weather appeared fine, and her father couldn't be persuaded at first. Finally, because she was so distraught over this man's death and this warning, her father did take his family off the island. His daughter begged him to, and they were all saved from a bad storm—the storm of 1822. Others were lost.

So the legend began that if the Gray Man appears to you before a storm you'll be saved. And also your property will be saved. There are all sorts of stories. Some who claim to have seen the Gray Man say he looks like an old man—the way Captain Bill described him. Others see him as a young man. The couple who saw him right before Hugo were a Mr. and Mrs. Moore, I believe. The beach houses on each side of them were totally destroyed. They walked back into their house in the midst of all this destruction, and the salt and pepper shakers and table setting were still in place. Nothing in their home had been disturbed. Uncanny. In fact, after Hurricane Hazel someone in a family had seen the Gray Man. Houses all over the island were destroyed, but that house still had their beach towels hanging on the railing. I saw pictures of that—the towels literally draped over the railing.

And you know, doing the *Unsolved Mysteries* program was fun. It all turned out rather interesting. They had the Captain Bill actor herding goats out on the beach because cows were too hard to find and manage. They needed a place for the young girl having her dream that a hurricane was coming, so we used the Hermitage, which was ideal. They needed a four-poster bed, which we had. They needed an old-timey bedspread. I had a hand-crocheted one that a cousin of my mother's had made, a lovely thing I never used. They had to make sure that the filming wasn't showing any electrical outlets. I helped with that and got a nice brass candlestick to make everything appear early 1800s.

You learn quick to see things in a new light—to approach a familiar old story and see it through the eyes of a film crew. I enjoyed the experience, and Georgetown County and Murrells Inlet got the national recognition that the Chamber of Commerce had hoped for. In fact, *Unsolved Mysteries* runs that film over again each year at about Halloween time. It's been nine years. When it first showed I got phone calls from people I hadn't seen in forty years saying, "I was in the kitchen and heard this voice on television and I thought that's Genny Chandler." They recognized my voice. They might not have recognized my face after that long. Friends I hadn't seen in forever got in touch, and that was fun. And now around Halloween time of each year I'm famous all over again. It's not the Gray Man who's been spotted. I'll go into the grocery store and the checkout person will say, "I saw you. You were on TV last night."

Alice Flagg

AND NOW AFTER REFUSING TO discuss Alice Flagg in front of a television audience, I'm going to discuss her in front of a book-reading audience—because as a retired librarian that's my prerogative. And anyway, being the most celebrated ghost on our coast, Alice Flagg is hardly a well-kept secret. Restaurants and everybody else use her name and image to sell, and more unfortunately, the young people have discovered a tombstone for an Alice Flagg at a local church and disturbed the spot with their constant attention. That's the wrong Alice Flagg, the wrong dates, and even the wrong cemetery.

Yes, I grew up surrounded by ghosts or at least that one ghost. When we were living at the Hermitage my older cousins kept June and me and my brothers scared to death. They were always talking about how the house was haunted, but back then the reference wasn't usually to Alice Flagg but to the "White Lady." My great aunt saw her. My great aunt was quite a bit younger than my grandmother. One was born before the Civil War and the other after. Aunt Lolly was visiting at the Hermitage. She was brushing her long dark hair sitting at the little dressing table, and in the mirror that she was facing she suddenly saw a woman dressed in a gauzy white gown. She whirled around, and nobody was there. She started brushing her hair again, and when she saw the image again she whirled around and threw her hairbrush. And her brush went right through this apparition and hit the wall. That was the story that we first heard associated with the Hermitage house. But then each of these old houses probably had a ghost of its own.

Actually, ghosts are in plentiful supply. Some people say that Cedar Hill parsonage, the house I live in now, is haunted because the builder,

Rev. James Belin, died here under slightly mysterious circumstances. He had come here as a missionary to the Negroes and Indians on Wacca- maw Neck but had a large white following as well. One afternoon when he was on his way to Wachesaw he was thrown from his buggy. No one was with him, so nobody knew why the horse ran away, but he was thrown against a live oak tree and died in this house on the same afternoon. So growing up, we always heard that the parsonage, which this is, was haunted. But I haven't seen or felt a ghost in this house, and if he's here I'm sure he's a kindly ghost, which in fact most ghosts are.

It's interesting. You never hear about a ghost harming a person. So why are we put off by the notion of ghosts? If a person believes in such, they shiver when they hear that a house is haunted. Yet never once have I heard of a ghost harming anyone. Oh, but when I was a child, just hearing a ghost story put goose bumps up and down my spine. I was scared to death. Now for Alice Flagg and myself.

As I said, growing up in the Hermitage I was always hearing about Alice Flagg—actually there are two stories. In one version Alice Flagg was voyaging to Charleston to attend school and she met and fell in love with the handsome young riverboat captain who was running the ship. In the second version the young man is a turpentiner. Taking sap from the pine trees was a big industry around here, but of course, neither of these occupations was quite upper-class enough. Nobody knows exactly which he was, but it is known that he came calling at the Flaggs' wanting to take Alice riding in his buggy. And Dr. Flagg, who had his horse saddled, said, "Young man, you take the saddle horse because you are much younger and more agile than I. You can ride my horse and I'll ride in the buggy with my daughter." I'm not sure what you can judge from that, but a lot of people say the Flaggs' pride was their downfall, both in dealing with Alice and in the even more fatal hurricane that came along forty years later.

Anyway, on one of these steamboat trips back to school in Charleston, Alice became very ill, and word was sent to Dr. Flagg to come and get her because the fever was contagious. The story is that

Dr. Flagg's son, Alice's older brother who was also a doctor, actually went and brought Alice home to the Hermitage. Then her father and brother, both being doctors, were tending her, and in the course of this they found that the girl had secretly been wearing a ring on a ribbon around her neck. They were disturbed by this—upset.

But I must tell you right now that I sincerely believe that my Uncle Clark started the business of Dr. Flagg being so furious that he threw this secret engagement ring in the creek. All that is completely ridiculous. My uncle invented the throwing away of the ring out of whole cloth and added it to the story. Dr. Flagg was a gentleman, and no matter how proud, he certainly would have returned the ring to the young man. So whoever the young man was and if there was a ring, for who can really know, he probably gave it to another girl.

Now back to the two versions that were around before Uncle Clark fiddled with the story: In one version Alice dies as her father finds the ring on the ribbon. But in the other version her brother, seeing how agitated she is over the loss of the ring, attempts to replace it with one of his own. And Alice, realizing what he has done, pulls his ring off herself, claiming she wants her own ring back. Either way, they say it's her missing ring that she comes to the Hermitage searching for.

How much of this story is true? I can't say, but I will tell you one thing for certain. If you grow up being told ghost stories—and our biggest entertainment was sitting in a darkened kitchen and being scared witless by Richard or Zacky Knox's storytelling or being out on the dock at night or up in my bedroom, which was called the "ghost chamber," and listening to our older cousins—well, for goodness sakes, you're going to see something. You can't very well spend years sleeping in a room called the "ghost chamber" and not see something sooner or later. Alice was supposed to have been very beautiful, so beautiful that they couldn't bring themselves to bury her. Of course, in those days keeping her too very long wasn't possible, and they did keep her a little longer than was practical and the casket was kept in June's and my bedroom. Still, that room could have also gotten its name because that was where my Aunt Lolly had seen the apparition standing behind her—the reflection in the mirror.

Plus, the Hermitage was almost a century old by then, and the doors sagged, the floors slanted, and the windows rattled. And we had moonlight filtering in through all sorts of cracks and drafts that matched whatever the wind was doing outside. Anyway, it's not surprising that I did have my own experience with Alice, a couple of experiences, in fact.

Once widowed Grandpapa (who was eighty) got in touch with his first sweetheart and they'd discussed marriage. He had even gotten a ring. Well, shortly before his death I came home from school one day and he told me to go over to his desk. This was in his bedroom, one of those old roll-top desks with all the drawers and compartments. He directed me to one pigeonhole in particular which contained a little box. He told me to bring it to him. Inside the box was this lovely gold ring, and since he wasn't going to get married again he wanted me to have it. I was fourteen and the ring was a bit loose on my finger, but I wore it all the time.

We Chandler children had gone out shrimping with the seine and filled up a washtub with shrimp that we brought home. Then I'd gone upstairs and was in my room alone, curled up in bed and reading a book which I held in one hand. Suddenly I felt a grip on my hand, the hand the ring was on, and as I jerked my hand away the ring flew off my finger and hit the floor. I jumped from the bed because I was sure my brother Tommy, the oldest of the three, had somehow played a trick on me. He loved to scare you. He'd hide behind the door and all sorts of things. I was certain Tommy was the culprit, but no one was in the room and he couldn't have gotten out the door. I ran downstairs, and there were Mama and the three boys in the kitchen heading shrimp. But I really didn't see anything. But the feel of that ring leaving my finger was pretty convincing. My bedroom was haunted.

Of course, having June for a sister didn't help either. One night we frightened each other with stories so badly that we kicked the foot out of the sleigh bed. We literally broke the foot of the bed kicking to get out of it we were both so frightened. Even in high school we acted this way. If we had friends spending the night, nobody ever slept. If we locked the door, the locked door would be open in the morning.

It was on one of those sultry summer nights before air conditioning, the kind where you'd give anything for a breath of fresh air. I heard the thunder rumbling and thought, Oh, thank goodness, rain. Well, June was playing the piano for a group of young people who, since it was summer, were probably from Marion. Back then young people would stand around a piano and sing songs. Everything in those days was either standing around the piano singing or telling ghost stories. I heard the thunder and walked out onto the porch. At the Hermitage the road came in from the highway and went up the creek edge to the front of the house. And between the creek and the house my grandmother had laid off a great circle drive. The circle was surrounded by oaks heavy with wispy moss and beyond that, of course, the gray marsh stretching out toward the beach.

As lightning flashed, I saw a figure on the road, but instead of coming toward the house, it appeared to follow the circle toward the creek front. That seemed strange in such a storm—that this person wouldn't be hurrying toward the shelter of the house. I got by the railing and, holding on, leaned out from the porch trying to see better. As the lightning flashed again there appeared to be a woman dressed in a long white flowing gown. This figure appeared to float. She moved without the motion of walking, just glided along.

I screamed. My brothers came running out onto the porch, all three of them, and I was pointing and shouted "Look!" And they said, "What?" The apparition had vanished. So, of course, to be brave they got a flashlight and said they would find her. But they didn't find anybody. The front yard was a peninsula, and it would have been difficult for a real person to have gotten off that point without being found. And there were no tracks showing the next morning, but the rain could have washed them away. In the end everybody decided that I saw Alice Flagg. I don't know.

Then (and this was quite a bit later) I was in college and home for the weekend. I had a paper due and was working the whole time. The kitchen was to the rear of the house and opened onto a back hall with a staircase that led upstairs. I heard Mama close the kitchen door as she was leaving that way, and then she let out a sound. Mama was not scary, not in the least. I'd never heard her scream or yell in my whole life. She sounded startled—she went "OOHHH." I jumped up and ran into the hall, and when I did I saw the figure. Mama was still at the kitchen door, and this figure, this woman, was close to her but beside the stairway. Mama said, "June," thinking this was my sister. Mama said, "June," again. And as Mama moved toward the woman, she just faded into the wall. Right in front of us both. She disappeared.

Now, Mama would never admit that anything had happened. She simply wouldn't. I don't know why. A little moonlight was coming through the windows on each side of the door of the back hall and the front hall. I suppose this figure could have been shadows. I do know I ran upstairs and June was asleep in her bed. June was eliminated.

Still, Mama was not going to admit she'd seen a ghost then or ever, but in an interview once she did comment on the ghosts of Brookgreen Gardens. What she said could have applied to the Hermitage just as easily, so I'm going to take the liberty of changing the noun. Mama said, "Ghosts? People who have lived in a place. Everybody has contributed something and there's some part of them that always stays with a house. Some destroy and some build it up but everybody contributes something. You're a part of everybody you've met, they say. And I believe that every house is a part of all the people who've lived there, don't you?"

My son, Jim, spent the night in this same house I live in now while it was being rebuilt. He was sure we had a ghost because he felt the room, as he said, "chill off just as if there was an air conditioner." The house was stripped down and didn't even have a fan. And a similar experience happened up at Fort Motte when he was a small child. His great-grandfather on the Peterkin side was Captain Jim, who was in the Civil War with the Confederacy, of course. We had a little portrait of him at the farm, one painted by a Frenchman who had served with him at Sullivan's Island. I don't know that my son, Jim, paid much attention to it, but the portrait was always hanging over the desk. One morning he said, "Mama, the strangest thing happened last night." He said, "I waked up and a tall man was standing right there in the doorway of my bedroom. He had on a uniform with brass buttons and a long dark beard." I said, "Jim, why didn't you call me?" He said, "Gosh, you would have run right through him to get in my room." He said, "I wasn't frightened. I just happened to wake up. I opened my eyes and he was standing there. When he saw that I saw him, he just smiled at me and sort of nodded his head and disappeared. It was like when I saw him that was all he wanted to happen."

But, you know, in all my years up at Fort Motte no one else besides my son ever talked of seeing a ghost in Confederate uniform. Jim was quite young then—maybe twelve.

School

AFTER SHE WAS MARRIED MAMA returned to teaching in the Inlet's two-room schoolhouse. In fact, when June was a baby, Lillie Knox brought her to the school at recess for Mama to nurse. Therefore, my sister got an early and extra exposure to schooling. But Mama used to tease me that I had the most education of any of her children. She was still teaching in that little school when she was pregnant with me and claimed I had eight and a half months of instruction before I came. I don't think it helped a bit. Six years later I entered that building for real, and there was June in the fourth grade and in the same room. That first grade was pretty miserable because June watched everything I did and then couldn't wait to jump off the school bus and tell Mama how I'd behaved that day.

But other than that, having four grades in one room wasn't so bad. In a way you learned faster because the teacher would start with us, the youngest, and then while we were doing our ABC's or learning script handwriting, she'd be teaching the second grade their reading and then spelling to the third and math to the fourth. By the end of the day the students were saturated with course work, their work and everyone else's.

One odd thing, though, was that when we went out to the playground, the boys had to march out to one side of the fence and the girls to the other. Boys and girls couldn't play together, but I remember that June had one little male friend who'd play catch with her across the fence. She would toss the ball to the boy's side, and he'd throw it back. And I remember how terrible children can be to each other. The older girls would tease one little girl by saying, "You have ancestors." She thought she had lice or something and would burst into tears.

From the second grade on I went to the Myrtle Beach schools because Mama felt they were better. That gave us a thirteen-mile bus ride, which wouldn't have been so bad except the one bus had to go both north and south. This meant that the Murrells Inlet children were gone dark to dark in the winter. A very long day, and while we did have plenty of "study time," we had no study hall and unless classes were in session, we were locked out of the school buildings even in the coldest weather.

I know it's an old saw to say "In my day we walked to school in the blizzard and you young people don't have it so bad." But things aren't quite so tough now. But some in the state still do have quite a bus ride, and I do get frustrated when I think that here I am seventy years old and education hasn't improved in South Carolina since I started school. I mean, it has, of course, and yet the state is still at the bottom in all the national testing, and that's because we've just never spent the money that we should on education.

I suppose my attitude toward our schools really comes from the fact that my school didn't offer all the required courses, and I had to go off to college at Coker on probation. The Myrtle Beach high school was doing as well as could be expected, especially considering the fact that the World War II airmen stationed there were marrying the teachers about as fast as they arrived.

Coker College had begun as a Baptist school for girls and was close by and had quite a good reputation—so good that girls came from the Northern states. And if she was from above the Mason-Dixon line, a student could literally have entered that college as a junior and done well, and I know that was because of high school preparation. Still, college was wonderful.

I planned to go two years at Coker for liberal arts and then two at the University of South Carolina in journalism. My English professor in high school had encouraged me, and I was awful at math. But when I got to Coker I was elected president of the freshman class, which threw me into student government. I was very bashful by nature, very reserved, and yet I was elected, and that set a pattern of serving in student government over the next four years (and for being interested in politics for the rest of my life). I got so involved and loved my professors and ended up graduating from there with a major in English literature and a minor in art and a minor in religion, which, of course, meant I wasn't fit to do any job on earth.

Still, these same professors had taught me something pretty basic, something I would have gotten at few other Southern schools—the ability to put myself in the place of others. I was taught that the Jim Crow laws were a disgrace and that a working man had a right to a living wage and a working woman had a right to that same wage—all notions that have served me well in the years since.

My senior year I did attempt to become a missionary, but they would only send me to China, and I wanted to go be a missionary in the South. I remember Mama coming home one day from her women's church meeting just fuming because they were taking up money to bring refrigeration to Africa and we didn't even have refrigeration in Murrells Inlet yet. No, going off to China made no sense. So, other than the desire to help, there I was with four years of college and no marketable skills.

I did love books, though. From my earliest years books had been my passion. Mama would read aloud to us five children every night— stories from the Bible, *Bulfinch's Mythology,* and Lord knows what else. We'd be sitting up in the boys' bedroom and my youngest brother, Bill, would go to sleep very quickly, so the next night Mama would start over at the point he missed until finally we memorized those passages, and to this day June and I don't like to be read to. But I was still the "reader" in the family.

When the Kimbels came to Wachesaw they gave us beautiful children's books and some with wonderful pop-up pictures. The story of Ping, a little duck in China. And I loved the Grimms' fairy tales. Books. June being the older sister and a teenager, as well, thought me a great annoyance and nuisance. When I was little she persuaded me that I was adopted because I didn't act like the rest of them. I always had my nose in a book.

My favorite place was a great big old yaupon tree, a bush really, but as big as a small live oak. It stood right on the edge of the creek at the Hermitage. The wind had blown that yaupon until the limbs had been bent over to form sort of a hammock—a perfect place to lie down if you were small, and I was. I'd climb that tree with a pillow and a book and spend the day up there. And June would be down on the ground fussing because I wouldn't come help her sweep out the house.

Ridiculous that she could persuade me that I was adopted because I did look so much like Mama. Except I did believe it. I fantasized. I read these wonderful fairy tales with princesses in castles, and I was sure I was supposed to be in that setting. I wasn't supposed to be in Murrells Inlet and be June's little sister. They had snatched me away from where I should have been.

Anyway, from fairy tales I graduated to Jane Austen, who was my favorite in high school, and I still love an English setting and manners and any novel that begins with something like: "It is a well-known fact that any man with a good fortune is in search of a wife." When I was fourteen I read *Forever Amber,* one of the best-known of the early "romance" novels. A girl in my class had gotten hold of her mother's copy. So shocking at the time and it's really nothing. But young ladies weren't suppose to read such, and we passed *Forever Amber* around and kept it hidden under our mattresses. In college Thomas Hardy just bowled me over—*Return of the Native* and *Tess of the D'Urbervilles* seemed so realistic to me—sort of the underside of life that no one around Murrells Inlet discussed.

Since college I've read mostly psychology and religion. But I do love books and I did want to have a life of helping others, so it's no accident that I ended up as a librarian—or not too much of an accident. Fortunately my adviser at Coker steered me in the right direction. She laughed at me for even considering a law degree and discouraged me from getting a teacher's certificate, saying once I had that certificate I wouldn't try anything else. Actually, I don't know if that would have been so bad, but she steered me to the nearby Conway library, and the librarian there, who was a very kind person as well as a fine librarian, encouraged me to go on to the University of North Carolina at Chapel Hill for a degree in library science.

At Coker I'd been an indifferent student, but at Chapel Hill you needed a B or better to stay in and you didn't even receive a grade until the end of the semester. That last was done to see how you dealt with stress, and the program was tough. Also Mama had sent me to college, and for graduate school I just couldn't let her keep paying. I borrowed the money, which along with a bit of maturity gave me the drive to do better. In short, I knew I was going to have to get a job in the future and pay back the loan.

The entire library school had only a couple of dozen students, but compared to Coker, Chapel Hill was very large indeed. A friend from high school gave me rides home, so I wasn't completely cut off from my earlier world, but still my horizons were broadening. This was in 1950, and Chapel Hill wasn't open to blacks. If memory serves, the Cosmopolitan Club was where we met and talked all this over—the notion of at least integrating the school on the graduate level. If black students wanted to go on to be doctors or lawyers or whatever, they had to leave the state. We signed petitions to change that. Issues like that mattered a great deal, and here, at least, we could give some voice to our ideas about justice.

Then I graduated and went out into the world.

Communism

THOSE PETITIONS I SIGNED IN graduate school came back to haunt me in a very strange way. Every morning when I went to class, I'd stop by the ladies' rest room and there'd be a copy of the communist newspaper the *Daily Worker* on the table. I don't ever remember reading it, but I was conscious that something called communism existed in the world and that I'd never encountered it in Murrells Inlet. At a much earlier date I read *Native Son* by Richard Wright. We had cousins in Columbia whom I visited, and when I was much too young I'd read *Black Boy* and *Native Son*. I didn't understand half of what I read, but in *Native Son* there were communists in Chicago and they were the "Reds." That was my first exposure to communism, and then I got to Chapel Hill and copies of the *Daily Worker* were lying around. My connection to communism was tenuous, to say the least.

But this was the time of McCarthyism. Two years after graduating I was in occupied Germany working as a librarian for the armed forces, and here came McCarthy's henchman, Roy Cohn, looking for communists. Four or five years ago I picked up a *Time* magazine and saw he'd died of AIDS. He was the first person I'd known who died of AIDS. Back then he was a young lawyer sent out to dig communists out of the military. We'd meet in the snack bar and have coffee in the mornings. I realized after I saw the *Time* article why he never asked me out on a date. Thank God he didn't, because I probably would have ended up going before McCarthy with the rest. I know that sounds ridiculous, but it's literally true.

Back home from Germany, I went to work at the Georgetown library. That was in 1954, and one morning a woman I worked with came in all excited and said, "Your friend was arrested yesterday and they've taken him to Washington to be questioned by the House Committee on Un-American Activities." I was frightened. The young man involved had been in our crowd at the Cosmopolitan Club where we'd signed all those petitions, and he'd been teaching here in little out-of-the way Georgetown, South Carolina, and been carried off to Washington, D.C. He was accused of being a member of the Communist Party while at UNC–Chapel Hill, a card-carrying member. But I hadn't known that. I thought, Dear Lord, what was I tangled up with when I signed all those petitions? I was saying that black graduate students should be allowed to attend Chapel Hill. That was the most progressive thing we'd signed as far as I could remember. Could they get me for that? I'd just returned from Germany where I'd had plenty of experiences with real communists—none of them pleasant. I had a brother in Korea fighting the communists.

Actually, all three of my brothers served in that war, but the oldest, Tommy, actually got over to Korea. I was in the theater watching the newsreel that came before the movie—the Movietone news. Tommy had wanted to be a frogman but ended up in the engine room of the USS *Begor,* a destroyer escort designated as APD 1 27. I was sitting in the dark, and up on the giant screen was the whole world seeming to blow apart. This Korean harbor was mined, and they were trying to evacuate the American troops. I suddenly saw the numbers APD 1 27 in the middle of these explosions. I couldn't even tell anybody in the family. I just had to wait until word came that his ship had been hit and the engine room did flood and that Tommy had narrowly escaped.

My brother had almost died fighting the communists. All I wanted was a fair America. That's how radical I was. And I doubt my classmate was much different, but just joining the Communist Party ruined that young man's life or at least finished his career. He lost his teaching job in Georgetown even before the hearing. Years later, when I was married and had my small son sitting in a car seat, I stopped at a drive-in in Myrtle Beach to get something cold to drink. Hot summertime, and in the car next to me was the man who'd been teaching in Georgetown and called to Washington. I got out and spoke to him. He told me he'd never been able to get another teaching job. He was working on a commercial fishing boat in North Carolina.

Germany

WHEN I WAS FINISHING UP at Chapel Hill, the dean of the library school recommended that I work for a while in the army's Special Services department. Well, I was young—too young actually. You had to be twenty-five, but they squeezed me in at twenty-three. Actually the dean talked two of us into going, but my companion went home to Kentucky on break and married a lawyer instead. Anyway, I wrote to Mama and told her, and she sent a postcard back saying, "Just what I would like for you to do."

I went, and looking back, I'm amazed I stuck with the program. I left Fort Bragg, North Carolina, in August of 1951. We were treated like military, at least when it came to travel, and I remember all the young servicemen on that train headed for Korea. They couldn't believe that I, by choice, was leaving home for Germany. And actually, Germany didn't turn out to be all that safe, but at least I wasn't going to Korea. Once in New York, I stayed over in New Jersey with the stone carver Robert Baillie, who was a friend Mama knew from working at Brookgreen, and when the ship was delayed ten days I was welcomed into this beautiful home with sculpture studio and garden attached. They were Scottish and still spoke with a brogue. Mr. Baillie's sister gave me a Bible to carry, and his wife carried me into New York City and bought me women's underwear, the long woolen kind she thought I would need in Germany.

Then I was on the USS *Buckner,* a troop ship. Twenty-some of us girls were on the top deck with a swimming pool and cruise ship accommodations and no men, for they were below. We could see them down there, and occasionally I would meet a serviceman in Germany and he'd say, "You had a red bathing suit. I saw you on the *Buckner*." That crossing took two weeks, and I made friends with the girls. In Nuremberg we got our orientation. That very first night the chief librarian of the U.S. Command gave a speech and said that one or more of us would be going to Bremerhaven. She made it sound like that girl, or girls, would be the "Miss America" of the crowd. She said it over and over again. "We will send the one we consider the most adaptable, the one we consider. . . ." Over and over we heard that. I was the lucky girl.

Bremerhaven was the outpost of the entire command and separated from the rest of the American Zone. You went by train. Bremerhaven was a seaport on the North Sea. Cold in winter. Very, very cold, but no snow. The first year I was there the base newspaper reported three days of sunshine—for the year. So dreary. It made you realize why the Scandinavians have such a high percentage of alcoholics. Dreary and depressing. In the winter the sun, what there was of it, was rising at eleven in the morning and going down at three. And that's why they made a big deal out of Bremerhaven, claiming that whoever went there was the pick of the litter. And, of course, we all realized that and were trying hard not to be that wonderful person.

When they announced I was the one going, I really could have cried. And yet once there I loved every minute of it. Despite that awful weather I got in with a great group of people. The post was a bit different in that the library was serving not just the army but the navy and the air force as well, so the library got a lot of use. But when I arrived I was warned about our boss, Major Wood. He was off on TDY, which stood for temporary duty something. They'd say, "Things are pretty relaxed now but just wait until Major Wood gets back from TDY." He came back after six weeks, and the morning he arrived I went to his office and shook hands with him. He sounded Southern, and when he put out his hand I spotted a Clemson ring. Clemson, as most sports fans already know, is a South Carolina university. He adopted me on the spot, he and his wife too. I really was too young to be over there and did need to be looked after.

Homesick soldiers! Poor boys would actually come up to the library desk and ask me to marry them. A corporal is definitely homesick if he wants to marry a librarian he met the day before yesterday. When I could afford it, on a day off I'd fry chicken and bake a pie for some of those boys. Never one at a time. Always a group. My roommate was from Ohio, and she thought I was an absolute idiot. She said, "You know, I grew up with my mother and father and sister, and we never once had a meal when there was someone else at the table." I said, "At my house mama said, 'count heads, set the table, and put on an extra place.'"

So that's what I accomplished in Germany. I had a children's reading program that I was very proud of and a little radio program, and I tried to be kind to homesick servicemen. But not too kind. As I said, my boss would check out my dates to make sure they weren't already married or wanted or anything else. He kept an eye on me, which was good because I was young and not equipped to deal with life over there. Definitely not a safe place if you were a fairly pretty twenty-three-year-old, and some married man or scoundrel could have easily fooled me. When I left there I went to Stuttgart. I didn't have that guardian angel around, but the chief librarian watched over me, and by then I had been there nineteen months and knew the ropes and had heard every line and many marriage proposals.

I didn't think much about that until my mother-in-law suggested I not marry her son because someone younger would come along eventually and want to marry me. I thought, My God, I've just spent those two and a half years in Germany saying "no, no, no."

As far as opening my eyes to the world goes, I had plenty of contact with the German people. All the staff working in the libraries were German, and since I had three libraries (and later five) to supervise I did meet them and grew fond of many. I suppose that's just my nature to like people, but also they were very much in need. They'd been through hard times, and I did sympathize. And yet, you occasionally came across this attitude—my secretary had been a member of Hitler Youth, and she was the one who said, "If Hitler was speaking tonight, I'd go to hear him."

One dear old man in particular was up past seventy and had been a librarian on a German cruise ship before the war. He was literally trembling the first day I met him. The previous librarian had been a young Jewish woman, and he felt she had hated him just for being German. Which was understandable, I suppose, but still that seemed like a strange job for that young woman to even want. It's hard to say who had actually done what during the war, who had participated actively in bringing about the Holocaust, who was aware of what. I got to know most of my workers and even went into their homes, and except for the woman who admitted she would attend a Hitler rally if it were held that night, most of them claimed that they knew nothing at the time. That's probably true of some. German soldiers weren't necessarily Nazis. The resistance had been eliminated over the years, and the German people really are followers and you could almost understand how Hitler sucked them in.

And yet. I got pneumonia and had to go to the hospital. My doctor told me he was a Nazi—had been and still was. He wanted to get to the States, and the quickest way was to marry an American. On my second day in the hospital he listened to my heart with a stethoscope, and on the third morning he came in and asked me to marry him. He scared me to death. I was so frightened I checked myself out. Actually, I just walked out of the hospital and still with pneumonia and called Major and Mrs. Wood, who rescued me. So I knew at least one other real Nazi.

Another time I'd gone to Hamburg for a weekend. I was walking alone but in uniform to the hotel, and a German man passed me on the street. Then he whirled around, came back, and began to spit on me. He was yelling, "Zie est Americanish, zie est Americanish zie stink!" One of the better lessons in my life—to realize for the first time, "He hated my guts because I'm American." Maybe his home was bombed. Maybe he lost his family. There's been severe bombing in Hamburg. Until that moment I couldn't imagine being hated just for being American. Of course, before I left Germany I was to hear plenty more on the subject of "Ami go home!" And today you take it for granted that Americans are hated. Just pick up a newspaper.

In the end, I suppose what was really disturbing about the German people, what really baffles me to this day, was in a book they kept in the library. This was an English translation of some of the articles published in German newspapers during the war, and reading them, it was difficult to see how any German could claim ignorance. I remember one reporter had gone to a prison camp on Christmas Eve and talked about what a wonderful thing the camp was doing for the country and how the people in there were not perfect and should be eliminated. Now, how could you read the newspaper and not tell what was going on?

As I said, what I can believe was that many German people knew but were hesitant because they were frightened. Because the Nazi threat had grown up slowly, they'd gone along and then were afraid to speak out. Reinhold Niebuhr, the great German theologian, wrote of how the Nazis first came for the Jews and no one spoke out. Then the Nazis took the handicapped and next the gypsies and no one spoke out. Then the Nazis came for the priests like him. By the time he decided to rebel it was too late. Before going to Germany, I'd actually worked for a year up in the Conway library. There in South Carolina the Ku Klux Klan had marched right through the streets of Conway. I remember my uncle saying, "There goes so and so." He recognized her from her shoes. I was shocked. I thought the KKK had faded out long before and truly didn't know it still existed. And I told the people who came through the library that I was shocked and how wrong I thought this was. I was living with my aunt and uncle, and my uncle told me if I didn't stop talking they'd come to our yard and burn a cross. And I got the same warning from the wife of a local lawyer. She said, "Miss Chandler, you have got to be careful how you talk about them. They meet in my husband's office every week." I certainly don't think this woman or my aunt and uncle were evil people, and yet it was so much simpler and safer to say nothing, to go along with your neighbors or, God forbid, your husband, and the same sort of thing to a much worse degree had happened in Germany.

Library Problems

I CAME HOME FROM GERMANY just before Christmas in 1953. I could have returned for another tour, but Murrells Inlet is a hard place to resist, especially at Christmastime, and I took a job as the head librarian in the nearby and brand-new Georgetown County library. The first real public library dated only from the WPA days, when Effie Thatcher and Mary Bonds opened one in the two-hundred-year-old Winyah Indigo Society building—paid for amazingly with bridge game benefits and the like. The "new" library came along in the early 1950s and was the refurbished old jail, which wasn't but one hundred years old. An excellent building, actually.

Georgetown is filled with beautiful old buildings, and the streets are truly shady and relatively quiet. I've always been fond of Georgetown. The people really are friendly and relaxed. And just being around books, I always enjoyed that, plus I was rooming in a house where I felt very comfortable and even loved. Still, this two years of my life were troubling in one respect.

Despite the recent Supreme Court decisions, the local library board had no intention of serving the black community. The army was integrated. The libraries in Germany had been integrated. The Georgetown library was being run on public money, and blacks were members of that public. I was only twenty-six and not nearly as forceful as I should have been. Still, I did continually bring this matter before the board and made a record each time a black patron was turned away from the library. They expected me to say, "I'm sorry, we don't have that book." That was ridiculous, but I agreed to say, "I'm very sorry but I can't help you," which, of course, was just as bad. This was so wrong to deny people books. In a way, locking away books was one of the biggest crimes of all. A good Catholic school was open to blacks, and the nuns asked me to help. I tried to start a branch library that would be open to all, but that didn't go through.

An interesting thing did happen, though. One day two men came into the library, one very tall and the other not. The shorter was quiet and just listened while the tall one asked questions. I showed them around the renovated old jail, and we discussed the integration of both the library and the schools. Then the shorter asked if I anticipated any language problems when integration finally did occur. I explained about the isolated communities like Sandy Island where the Creole language of Gullah was still being spoken. That would be a hard adjustment for both black students and black teachers.

Now, both of them spoke with strong English accents, and when I asked, the taller said he was from Australia and the shorter said South Africa. And I said, "If there was one person in this world I could meet, it would be the South African novelist Alan Paton. I have just finished reading his *Cry, the Beloved Country* and thought it the greatest book I ever read." The taller man said, "That's the way we feel about him in my country too." The shorter man just bowed his head. So we talked on. The shorter one did finally say that they were traveling through the South for *Collier's* magazine and doing an article on the difficulties that this region would face with the integration of the public schools. He told me that in South Africa many of the tribes had their own distinct languages, which made it difficult to even bring the black people together—much less the blacks and whites. Then they left.

About three weeks later I was home sick with the flu. A friend brought by a copy of a *Collier's* magazine, and there on the cover was a picture of Alan Paton. He was the shorter of the two men and hadn't said a word while I was raving about his talents. And the problem of the Gullah language did get mentioned in the article.

But other than that very brief encounter and my rather passive resistance I didn't accomplish anything toward integrating the system.

After two years I quit to get married, then had a child the next year, and then ran into an almost identical problem where we were living a hundred miles upstate in Calhoun County. While I was visiting on the coast, up there they shut down the library completely. Young blacks had tried to check out books. I was on the library board and went to the next meeting and spoke out. Our senator was furious with me. He expected the Justice Department to investigate, and he was telling us what to say. When I refused to go along, he said, "Mrs. Peterkin, I cannot conceive of a Southern white lady thinking as you do." Actually he said "Southern woman" because I'd given up my ladyship status. I said, "If we don't resolve this problem right now my one-year-old son will end up meeting in some group when he's a grown man trying to figure out how to bring a public library to this community." You see, now I was a mature matron of twenty-nine with a child and could stand my ground. And that argument finally did prevail, and after many, many years that angry senator did become my friend. They couldn't close that library for all eternity. Nothing down here on earth lasts forever.

MARRIAGE

Bill Peterkin

IN THE 1893 HURRICANE THE kitchen wing had washed off the Buck's Inlet house and came to rest lodged in the live oak tree right next door. That kitchen was just one big room with a door and a window or two. And this lot on the mainland it floated to happened to belong to Henry Buck, who I believe was a distant cousin by marriage. Grandpapa bought the lot, got the kitchen for free, and put a porch around the whole business.

Because the storm had washed over it with saltwater, the beach we call Garden City today was full of dead live oaks and dead cedar trees lying like skeletons in the sand or still standing upright. Grandpapa just cut the limbs off some of these, left the stubs showing, and those were the porch posts. As I mentioned earlier, very rustic.

The Bates house, which is nearby and still standing, had a roving history as well. Before the hurricane Dr. Allard Flagg had started building a house over on the beach. The black people told him his house would never stay there. The Lord would take it away because he had torn down St. John the Evangelist, an abandoned Episcopal church over at Richmond Hill, to get his timbers. The blacks said, "You won't get a house out of God's timbers. The Lord will take it away." And He did. The hurricane of 1893 came along and washed it away before they finished. But like the Buck kitchen, a lot of the timbers washed up right here, and the Johnson family used them to build their summerhouse.

And my grandfather's brother Ed Willcox built a house in the same manner. I remember as a child climbing on those cut-off limbs of the porch piling. You could say that much of the early construction in Murrells Inlet was a gift of that great and terrible storm, so I guess in a way so was my husband, Bill. That house my grandpapa made out of the Bucks' kitchen he sold to my husband's father. Not that I wouldn't have known Bill Peterkin anyway, because like everyone else in the South we were distant cousins—but it was quite convenient to have him summering only a few doors down. That was propinquity. We'd always been close by each other, except in our ages.

My first memory of Bill was when I was eight years old. A group of us children were swimming off Luther Smith's dock, the place where he tied up the old *Ann Howe,* the deep-sea fishing boat Luther had built himself. An outboard motor boat was a rare thing in those days, a very rare thing. And one came by, what we would have called a speedboat. Some adult standing on the dock said, "There goes Bill Peterkin in his new boat."

That's my first memory, but oddly enough I don't recall seeing or hearing about him again until I was eighteen. I'm sure he was around, but it just doesn't register. His mother, Julia, came most every summer, and Mama would have supper at her house. The summer I was eighteen I was invited as well. And before we started the meal Bill came into the living room, and I thought, "Now there's a really fine man." He was quite a bit older than I, but I had this vague notion that I was fortunate to have him for a distant cousin. He looked like someone I'd like to be kin to. He graciously apologized for missing supper. He was a widower by then and had a date in Myrtle Beach. He was twenty-four years older than I—almost a world of difference.

I didn't see Bill again for a long time. I'd returned from Germany and was working at the Georgetown library. I'd gotten together with a few other people and organized the Murrells Inlet Protective Association because they were planning to dredge a channel in back of the Garden City Beach from the inlet all the way to the causeway. Right through the marsh. They wanted a canal. Incidentally the "they" in this case was mostly locals wanting to build marinas and run deep-sea fishing boats, my brother Tommy being included here. The summer people were mostly the ones objecting. Anyway, our side had a notion—a hunch—that the salt marsh would be damaged and our lives would be irretrievably altered.

Anyhow, my future husband, Bill, and his mother joined our Protective Association, and they'd stop by the house and pick up Mama and me to go to the meetings. Our shared interest just brought us together. One evening that winter my mother said (she was probably the age I am now), "Sis, I can't bear to die and leave you an old maid." Well, my whole family had given up on the idea that I would marry. I liked my work at the library, was very happy there. I had thought I was in love a number of times, which I obviously was not since I didn't marry. So one evening Mama just came out in this very sad voice. "I just can't bear to think I might die and leave you alone." I can't imagine saying this now, but I answered, "Mama, if I could just find a man like Bill Peterkin, I would want to marry." But it never occurred to me that I would marry him. First of all, he was far too old. I was twenty-seven.

Of course, as Mama was pointing out, in my generation you were an old maid at twenty-five, so I was over the limit already. (Of course, she was ignoring the fact that she'd married at thirty-two.) Some of my old college friends came for a visit recently, and we talked about what our generation had just accepted without a hint of rebellion. We were idiots. A girl went to college, and boy, if she didn't have a diamond by her senior year so she could get married in the month of June, she was a failure. Finding a husband was the only aim of being at college—of even being on this planet—and marriage was all a girl had to look forward to. That is so wrong, so terrible. But women didn't work the way they do today. World War II changed that. Just as it started opening the South up, it gave women the kinds of jobs they'd never had before. But that change was slow in coming to South Carolina, very slow. The fact that so many marriages made it—and many, many made it—is just fine, but women had no alternative. And whatever job college had trained them for usually went untried.

Now, at that time we didn't have any telephones in private homes. The grocery store had one. When I was growing up, a telephone message had to be bad news because someone would drive up from the store all the way to the Hermitage and announce that Mrs. Genevieve had a call and that the number for her to come to the store and call was such and such. Of course, you knew someone was either dead or dying. Always some sad message from a relative that lived somewhere else or otherwise they'd have just written a letter. But even when we got our own phone that ringing still produced a feeling of anxiety. Still does. You can't get rid of what's been ingrained in you since childhood.

So this was in 1956 and we had no telephone in the house. Young men who were friends of mine would come down to the Inlet and just stop by. If I didn't have a date, they'd say can you go over to the pavilion tonight? Or whatever we might be doing. On the Fourth of July— on the Fourth everybody came to the Inlet or to the beach—June was home. I was in my bedroom. She and I had been in the creek, and I'd gotten the first shower and was getting dressed. June came up and said, "Sis, so and so is out there." She named some young man I knew from Marion. Then in a few minutes she came back and said, "And now so and so is down there." Then another caller showed up, and finally I just wanted to stay in the bedroom because four of them were waiting. And I knew I'd have to go out and tell them all I was busy and couldn't go out that evening.

Then June came in the bedroom and said, "Bill Peterkin just came up and wants to see if you'd like to go fishing." Well, recently Bill had taken me out fishing in this eighteen-foot boat he'd built himself and named the *Queen Mary*. And I did the craziest thing. I walked out on the porch, went up to Bill Peterkin, put my hands on his shoulder, and kissed him on the cheek. And he was furious. As soon as the others had gone, he said, "Don't ever do that again unless you mean it." And I knew what I had done. I had used him. I had indicated to the rest that they could just go. And they had all disappeared in a hurry. I mean, I didn't consciously set out to do that, but I understood his anger. The fact was I wanted to go fishing with Bill Peterkin. That was the Fourth of July, and we were married on the 15th of October.

I suppose I prodded him along by saying the army library service had offered me a job in Alaska. But that wasn't really necessary. Even before he proposed Bill would say things like, "I think you and my son would be friends." And he had talked about why he hadn't married again. Bill's son William was four when his mother died, and his grandmother Julia had really been the boy's mother. Julia herself had had a stepmother, and she really did consider stepmothers evil. And she had ingrained that in Bill, who otherwise would probably have been married long before and not to me. But now William was nineteen and in the navy and no longer in need of a mother (though in the years to come I suppose I would be at times). Anyway, William was stationed in Honolulu and came home that August for a visit. We all went fishing together, and I got to know him a little better.

Soon after, in early September, Bill came by the library when I was closing up. I had locked the door, and he pulled up in front, got out of the car, and said, "There's something down the road I want to show you." I asked, "What?" And he said, "I don't want to tell you. I want to show you." There was no way for me to let Mama know I'd be home a little later than usual. Our lives had a normal order to them that didn't allow for such sudden excursions, and she'd be worried when I didn't show up at home. But I got in Bill's car anyway and started going south, crossing the Sampit River Bridge. Murrells Inlet was north, and I told him I had to at least go in the direction of home. But he repeated, "Oh, it's not far. I just want to show you something down the road." Then we passed that beautiful old box of a plantation house at Hopsewee and crossed the broad marsh delta of the Santee turning golden now in autumn and the fading light. I said, "We're going to Charleston?" And he said, "No, nowhere near Charleston." Then he turned on the road leading to Hampton Plantation, which was where the state's poet laureate Archibald Rutledge lived, the one I quoted earlier at Brookgreen, and I thought he meant to show me this great columned house with live oaks covering the lawn, but he said, "No, not Hampton." And he turned down a long, narrow, straight, sand road and there, in the middle of nowhere, was this handsome semi-abandoned church I had never seen before.

We got out and he said, "I just wanted you to see this church. That was so strange for Bill. He was not a "churchy" person at all. He was a deeply spiritual person, but not one to show interest in such a building. This was St. James Santee Episcopal Church. It dated from colonial times and hadn't changed a bit since construction. The front columns were round and of brick. All was of brick, ancient and weathered. Outside under the oaks and giant pines the tombstones were propped and partly tumbling, and then we walked inside and saw these deep cypress pews, twisting and turning in odd conformations. And that late autumn light was coming through the doorway and the loose shutters of the windows. So very strange. We walked in there, and he asked me to kneel down there in front of the altar and this dark wood railing, and he knelt down beside me and asked me to marry him. So through all our marriage, if I ever was really angry, I would say, "You tricked me, damn it." I mean, what woman could say no to that proposal?

Marriage and a Child

Now we were engaged. Of course, Mama was happy. She'd been a great admirer of Bill's grandfather Dr. Julius Mood. He had a good boat called the *Nancy* which could be taken offshore to fish, and she was often their guest. Mama made those trips with Dr. Mood. And she had a little boat called *The Smiling Sally* that she would row over to the Moods' house. She would sit on the steps as a teenager and listen to him talk. He was a brilliant man, and she was fascinated. I believe Mama lined up the men in her life as God first, Daddy second, and Dr. Mood third, which no doubt is why sentences like "Bill Peterkin is the only man who is good enough for you" had popped out of her mouth. She thought Bill was a lot like his grandfather and therefore qualified to marry her daughter.

Mama suggested Thanksgiving Day for a wedding because she'd been married on that day in 1922. But Bill said no because his father's funeral was on a Thanksgiving Day. A day happy for Mama and sad for him, so the date was pushed up a couple of weeks. And there was the advice of Wallace Heyward, who as a young man had promoted himself from Cousin Julia's fish cleaner to cook and who advised Bill to marry on a Monday. You always started off something new on a Monday. He told Bill that and told me that Bill was only marrying me so he'd have Wallace on one end of the bait seine and me on the other—which might have some truth to it 'cause when you need live bait for winter trout that water is very, very cold.

But beside debating the when of the wedding we were also debating its shape. Bill had already been through a large wedding and I knew he'd be happy with something small and I would be. I'd been the May

Queen and worn plenty of pretty white gowns in college. June was expecting her third child, and so as a convenience to her we planned on a wedding at her house in Columbia with her and our immediate families in attendance. Then suddenly Bill announced that he'd be cutting soybeans in early November. He said, "Why don't we get married today?" I was stunned, but my mother was home from work so we went to Myrtle Beach and got a wedding ring and then went to Prince George Church and got married in the middle of October 1956.

Bill sent a cablegram to his son, William, who was on a ship in the Pacific, and his captain called him in to deliver the message. The captain said, "Son, I knew damn fool things happened in the South, but it looks to me like your daddy has married his sister." I guess my identity had officially changed a bit. Besides being Mrs. Peterkin, I became "Sister" to husband and stepson and the rest of the world. Until then I'd been Genevieve everywhere but in the home. I'd started as Little Sister until I reached twenty, and then my family condensed me to plain Sister, and ever since my marriage I've been Sister to all I've met and all I knew before.

Except to my mother-in-law, Julia. The Peterkins and the Chandlers were distantly related to begin with, so we'd always called each other Cousin. Now having Cousin Julia for a mother-in-law did present a truly serious problem. I remember a friend in Georgetown, on hearing of the engagement, said this, "My God, how do you think you can possibly get along with Julia?" A lot of people felt that Bill had been a widower so long and living with his mother all that time and she wouldn't accept a new wife. And it was difficult for her. But I had the advantage of growing up in a home with a difficult grandfather, and I'd learned to respect age and accept a bit of contrariness. I didn't buck age. And I did win Julia over, and she did love me. And I understood her, which made returning that love easy—all of which was fortunate since we were living in the same house.

Now, when I was in college, we came to biology class one day and our teacher, Dr. Matthews, was so excited over a new discovery. And she told us about positive and negative blood types, explaining that if a woman had negative blood and her husband had positive blood and the child they conceived had the husband's blood type, there could be a problem. A woman might have two children without difficulty, but after that a danger to the fetus certainly existed.

I remembered that biology lecture but didn't realize I had negative blood until I gave blood during the Korean War. Even then I wasn't alarmed for I could have at least two children. Soon after marriage I became pregnant, recalled all this, and told my doctor. He thought I had nothing to worry about with this first child. What neither he nor I knew was that the transfusion I'd been given after Daddy died had already sensitized my blood. That was back when they thought I was anemic and had brought the boys from the football team over and given me a direct transfusion that sent me into shock and nearly killed me.

Anyway, I was expecting Jim and didn't anticipate any problems. The day he was born happened to be a Saturday. My doctor, Rouse Huff, was a great person whom we all loved, a general practitioner, which was getting rare even back then. He delivered Jim and knew immediately something was wrong. But he didn't know what. When you look back on life there are so many miracles that we don't recognize as miracles when they're occurring. A new pediatrician had just moved to Orangeburg, and because this was Saturday he was playing golf. My doctor sent for him. Jim was just a matter of minutes old, and this doctor whom I'd never seen before ran into my room. He said, "Mrs. Peterkin, have you ever had a blood transfusion?" I said, "Yes. Why?" But he flew out of the door, and I still didn't realize there was a problem because Jim had looked fine in the delivery room or at least looked fine to me. Actually, he was extremely jaundiced. In a moment here comes my husband, Bill, and the new doctor back into the room, and this strange doctor is saying that he'll attempt to save our baby's life but he's never done an exchange transfusion before, which would be the only way he could go. "We don't have time to find a donor," he said. "There's some O negative in the blood bank, and O will mix with any type." But he'd never done this without a live donor. Everything was wrong, but at least he had seen this type transfusion performed in medical school. He told me all that and then explained all the possibilities. A child with severe brain damage. No sight. No hearing.

Such awful possibilities, but Bill and I both said the same: "Try and save him." Oh, we tormented that baby during his first year. We had a little music box we'd play on one side of the crib and then the other to see if he noticed the sound. And we were forever waving objects in front of his eyes. We just pestered him until he began to grow and we finally realized he was fine. He did have to go back to the hospital for more transfusions that first year, though. And his development at first was very slow since his body had to start manufacturing its own blood.

Jim grew up just fine, a bright child with perfectly good sight and hearing. When he finished kindergarten, the teacher came up to the car on the last day. She knew about Jim's problems at birth, and she said, "Sister, I don't usually comment to parents, but I give a little test to judge how students are prepared for the first grade. Jim had the highest score." I just started crying. She said, "I didn't tell you that to make you cry." Oh, such feelings. Twenty years later when Jim died in a boating accident, the dear doctor who had delivered him came up at the funeral and said, "Sister, he was always my miracle boy and we weren't supposed to keep him."

Bill Hickman

SMALL TOWNS HAVE A TOLERANCE for eccentrics and generally odd behavior and alcoholism, too, that I'm not sure you find in big cities. You do see pictures of all those homeless sleeping on the pavement and wandering around between the skyscrapers, but I'm not sure that's the same thing. There's a tiny sand spur crowded with stunted live oaks and cedars just inside the mouth of the inlet called Drunken Jack Island, and the story goes that when the pirates came ashore to bury their treasure one of them named Jack got drunk, wandered off, and was marooned. His skeleton was discovered years later clutching a rum bottle. Well, that's just legend. The truth is just as strange. Early in the nineteenth century a self-proclaimed preacher, what Mama used to call a "yard ax" preacher, would row out to that island to go on a drunk. When the urge for demon rum was under control, he'd row back. His name was Jack.

Bill Hickman was sort of in that tradition, only more so. He came here in the late 1930s and built a lean-to on my grandfather's land, just a bit to the south of where I'm living now. The land was all woods, totally woods. He took pine saplings and built right on the creek front, and nobody knew he was there. He hadn't cut his hair and had a very long scroungy kind of beard, just bushy all over, but nobody knew he was living among us. Well, my little brothers would take their red wagon and go to find pine knots for kindling. And they'd hunt for birds and squirrels with their BB guns. They saw Bill Hickman moving through the bushes, thought he was a bear, and shot him with their BB guns. That was Bill Hickman's introduction to our community.

Nobody ever knew exactly why he was with us. One story was that he had accidentally killed his own brother. This drove him crazy, and he left his home in the vicinity of Tabor City, North Carolina, and wandered here. Whatever the truth, he was a real hermit and stayed one all his life, but he was a hermit who would be around people occasionally and enjoyed annoying them. I guess it was a teasing of sorts. I'd been married a while, and Jim was about eighteen months old. I was holding his hand and walked up to the door of a new fish market. This was summer, and we'd come down to visit. Bill Hickman was sitting on a stump at the entrance. Bill says, "Tell me, Sister, did you ever get married?" Of course, that alone was an insult since I was holding the hand of what was probably my own child. I said, "Of course, I did, Bill. This is my little boy, Jim." He said, "Well, I'm glad to hear you're married 'cause you wouldn't have a chance no more."

The storekeeper, Danny Eason, came flying out the door swinging a broom at Bill and saying, "You get off my property. You can't insult ladies like that." I said, "Oh, Danny, leave him alone. I know Bill Hickman." Let me say in all modesty that I was a handsome enough woman and had no reason to take him seriously, and yet I remember that tease to this day. But maybe that was just payback.

Some years before, my brother Tommy and one of his friends had come across Bill Hickman passed out in the dead marsh grass along the creek bank. He'd do that—drink, pass out, and lie there until he sobered up. So there he was laid out in what Tommy figured were the same clothes he'd been wearing for almost twenty years. Tommy and his friend went and bought some new jeans and a white shirt. While he was still out they cut his hair, shaved off his beard, sponged him off, and dressed him in the new clothes. Oh, when Bill Hickman came to he thought he'd been mistaken for dead and laid out for his funeral. He was furious and swore to kill whoever had done that to him. He would have too, but nobody told, at least not then.

Small-town life is strange in its tolerances. Finally the community got together to build him a house. He'd been living in a lean-to for so long the Grant family volunteered a site and collected up money. Everybody gave something, and the local men did the labor. And for all that,

Bill insisted on a one-room cabin with no windows and one door. A very small shack back in the woods was his idea of the perfect home.

Captain Peterkin

FORT MOTTE, MY HUSBAND'S COMMUNITY, was a place that came with a great deal of historical baggage—a spot that had almost an ironclad tradition of public service and sacrifice. Secretary of State John Foster Dulles's ancestors had a cemetery there. Speaker of the House Langdon Cheves had his home there. And, of course, my mother-in-law, Julia Peterkin, was still in residence. Besides winning the Pulitzer Prize for her writing, she was best known as a social activist, most particularly as a member of the Anti-Lynching Society. But I should start at the beginning.

An early resident of this neighborhood was Rebecca Motte. During the Revolutionary War the British commandeered her strategically placed home—a bend of the Congaree River where that river and the Wateree come together to make the Santee. From here they could control all the waterway traffic coming from upstate, and the partisan general Francis Marion wanted them out. He surrounded the house but the British wouldn't surrender, so Rebecca opened a trunk and offered Marion the arrows that her brother had brought back from his travels in the South Seas. They were arrows whose ends could be lit. She told Marion to burn the British out—to burn her own house down.

Marion's men shot the arrows, and the British surrendered. Actually there are two endings to this story. In one they got such a hot and wonderful fire that the Americans and British sat down and roasted sweet potatoes and had supper together. In the other ending both sides joined together, put out the fire, and saved the house. Either way, a DAR monument to Rebecca Motte is on the site.

Then right next door was the Confederate captain my son, Jim, had dreamed of, the one whose small portrait hung over my husband's desk. Bill's grandfather, Capt. Jim Peterkin, bought Lang Syne after the Civil War. He was over in Marlboro County but had served in the Confederate army with a couple of men from the Fort Motte area. They talked about the rich clay land here, and in 1870 he sold his farm and moved to Lang Syne, which was the place at Fort Motte.

Now, Captain Peterkin was actually a major, but he'd demoted himself to captain. That's an interesting story. He was in his late twenties when the war started, and he outfitted a group of young men from Marlboro County as a cavalry unit. That's how it was done in those first days of the Civil War. Most of these were boys, sixteen or seventeen, so he was the old man and the leader. They were in service a long time and finally ended up at Sullivan's Island down on the edge of Charleston Harbor. He got a message from General Hampton saying he needed the horses of the unit but not the men. And Captain Peterkin, who was actually a major then, knew his men wouldn't be happy about losing their horses to another cavalry. So he actually locked his own men up in the stockade to get the horses away to send to General Hampton.

Of course, he had done the right thing. He was looking after the cause instead of himself and his unit. But those men of his never forgave him for making infantry out of them. They became infantry and he demoted himself to captain. When I say he chose to leave Marlboro County, that's not exactly the whole truth. Those young men never forgave him for taking their horses. After the war his barns were burned, so he left under duress and came to the Lang Syne portion of Fort Motte. At least that's what one of his grandsons told me.

While Captain Peterkin was on Sullivan's Island he did help his neighbors, though. He had access to the shipments of blockade runners, and if the Marlboro people needed medicine he would get it for them. But that didn't cancel out taking away the horses. And I believe he may have been some kind of spy toward the end of the war, because he told my mother-in-law he'd worn a Northern uniform at times. And he also told her that any man who did his duty in that war wouldn't talk about it later, so these stories have been patched together from his short remarks and other sources.

Once he was on a train in Richmond, Virginia, and attached were boxcars full of caskets. He claimed that he happened to be walking through and saw the name of his brother on one. So he stayed on the train all the way home to make sure his brother could be buried in Marlboro County. Oddly, that same metal casket turned up in a horrible way, for when they were building a highway it was unearthed. A man from the funeral home called and asked if I'd like to buy some pictures he had taken of the mummified body. I thought he was sick, which he was. But there's another odd story connected with that trip that's sort of romantic, or at least dramatic.

While Captain Peterkin was home delivering the coffin, before he could get back to Virginia and his unit, some of Sherman's scouts showed up. Someone warned him to leave—to run. He had a beautiful pocket watch, the largest pocket watch I've ever seen—as big around as a Baby Ben. He took off in the swamp behind the house and waded, but before he went into the water he hung that watch on the rail of an old fence post. Then he waded out and stood in the midst of the cypress knees to hide. A young Yankee soldier came up to the bank and spotted the watch. But Captain Peterkin had his rifle aimed right at him. The young soldier peered around in the thicket, saw Captain Peterkin, and raised his own rifle. At which time Captain Peterkin said, "If you shoot, we'll both be dead." The young soldier thought about it a moment and then turned and walked away, leaving both the watch and the Confederate. I'm told this is a bit like the ending of that popular novel *Cold Mountain,* except in that the young soldier shoots the hero and then walks away.

Odd to say, a story from my mother's side of the family occurs in the same neighborhood as the watch incident. Mama's mother was born in 1860, so she was a little girl then. She was sitting on the fence in front of her home. Her daddy was John Moore, and he'd left college at Chapel Hill and gone to war. My granny was sitting on the fence, and some of the scouts from Sherman's army came through—what they called "bummers"—just taking whatever they could get their hands on. Stealing. The scouts reined up in front of her house, and one said, "Little girl, where's your pa?" And she answered, "Pa's off killing Yankees, but grandpa's in the swamp hiding cows." They spent a lot of time out there in the swamps, but I'll let Aunt Hagar and Ellen Godfrey finish that subject up in the next chapter. And in a couple of chapters beyond that I'll return to Fort Motte and that sense of duty.

Aunt Hagar

"JESUS! WE HAD A SERMON yesterday! Mother's Day! Mother's Day all over the world! That man preach! He preach Mother's Day. He ring down on Mother's Day. Mother teach your children right. I declare that man preach Mother Day till he preach me out of my senses. I know I won't be here another Mother's Day. I got to move and shout! Say, Mother Day, again, I ain't here! I tote the baby in my arms. Rachel's own. I got the child. But I had to pitch up! Rachel call: 'Get that child from Grand Ma! Get 'um before Grand Ma drop him!'

"Fire take that church. Heart commence to turn over! I say, 'Take this child! Take 'um!' Rachel take her baby. I rose up for Mother and that suit of white. Great Lord! The whole thing been jump! Fire take that house. The Lord's Spirit filled the church. Now Easter holding the baby. You know I want to rush to her. She calls me kin. I hold out my hand and say, 'Jehovah, I depend on you!' I look on Easter. She a motherless and a fatherless child. Oh, them children!" That's Aunt Hagar describing a Mother's Day church service for Mama's benefit—for the benefit of the WPA collection. Aunt Hagar Brown was from the Wachesaw community, and once we'd moved to the seashore she'd walk over at least once a week. Lillie would fix her breakfast, and she'd stay for an evening meal as well. Even after Daddy died we had a cow which the first thing each morning Lillie would milk. Mama always gave Aunt Hagar two quarts of milk in two quart jars, and Lillie would fill her sack with what Aunt Hagar called her "visions"—her provisions. She would put in a little coffee and tie a knot in the sack, and then enough grits for the week and tie a knot, some fatback and tie a knot, and then Mama would put those two quarts of milk in her hands. Most of the time

Mama would drive her home, but the few instances she couldn't, Mama would say, "Poor Hagar, by the time she walks home she'll have butter-milk." And that sack Aunt Hagar had on her back looked like a sausage. That's all that old lady was going to have for the week except what she grew in her garden and the eggs from her chickens.

Oh, but when Aunt Hagar stepped into our house, no matter what time of day, she'd put her hands in the air and say, "Lord, bless this house and keep the soul!" I didn't understand until many years later that this was a traditional African greeting. "May this house be safe from tigers" was the African version one traveler brought back. Fortunately, we didn't have to worry about tigers.

That was Aunt Hagar, and I'm including her here for a reason. She'd been born into slavery. She was very young then but she remembered, and my mother interviewed many others who also remembered. And my mother was one of the few interviewers who was trusted, so what she was told was almost always an indictment of slavery. And, of course, I was always tagging along behind Mama. It's odd, for I realize my gen-eration is the last who will have this direct link—of actually hearing all this. I'm told that the slave interviews conducted by Genevieve Willcox Chandler are now available on the Internet, which is wonderful, but still not a substitute for traveling in a rickety old car down those nar-row sandy roads through the pine barrens and arriving at a cabin where a woman who has actually been freed by the Yankees waits with a pipe in her mouth and her skirt spread about her on the porch. And she tells you her story. This is Aunt Hagar speaking on the work done in the rice fields and a bit more. A "task" was the amount of work a slave was expected to do in a day—usually an amount of acreage that they would cultivate in a single day—a half acre if they were cutting. A "ration" was the food allowance each family received. And, of course, "Reb Time" meant before the Civil War was lost and freedom came.

> In the Reb Time, you know, that's when they sell you all about.
> Massa sell you all about. You broke through them briar and branch

and thing if you want to go to church. Sneak to church. Them patrol get you. The church Old Bethel. You don't know them. That building been gone.

I hear my ma say, "I too glad my children ain't been here Rebs Time! Give you task. You rather drown than not done that task!" Ma say, "Auntie poor weak creature. She couldn't strain." Ma had to strain to fetch her sister up with her task. There in the rice field. Ma say, "We on flat boat going to the island. See cloud, pray God send rain!" When rooster crow, she say they pray God to stop the rooster. Rooster crow, broke up the weather. When rooster crow scare them 'cause the crowing make the rain stop. Ma say, "We drag the pot in the river when the flat going across." They do this to make it rain.

Massa! You don't done you task, driver wave that whip. Put you over the barrel. Beat you so blood run down! I wouldn't take 'em. Ma say, "I too glad my children ain't born then."

Ain't no cash money for the slave. Where you going get them. Only cash is the Gospel. You have to get the Gospel. They give you cloth. Give you ration according to how many children you got. One time the children feed all the corn to the fowl, all the ration. Children say, "Papa love he fowl. Papa love he fowl. Three peck a day. Three peck a day." Parent come to the door. Not a grain of corn left. Poor people. Not a grain left to eat. But everybody on the hill help. Everybody on the street. One give this. One give that. You handle the vital light they last you until Saturday and then get ration again.

When Ma get down, she very sick. She say, "I going to leave. I gone leave here now. But, oh, Hagar. Be a mother and father for Katrine."

I say, (I call Katrine Gob). I say, "Better tell Gob to look after me!" I nothing but a child.

Ma say, "When I gone I ask the Master to send a drop of rain to let true believer know I gone to Glory."

When they lift the body to take 'em to the church, rain go "Tit! Tit! Tit! Tit!" on the house. At the gate moon shine out.

Ellen Godfrey was another who remembered slavery. A small band of Union soldiers had landed, and several were captured. One of these was hanged by the Confederates, and a slave as well. In retaliation the Union gunboats fired on the nearby plantations. At that point the planters put their slaves on flat boats and hid them deep in the swamps—in the same sort of inland swamps where Bill's Peterkin grandfather and my great-grandfather Moore had hidden out. In fact, the slaves were taken by way of Major Drake's plantation, and Drake was Bill's great grandfather. Maum Ellen was one hundred when she gave Mama this account of traveling with and cooking for those refuges.

Flat 'em all up to Marlboro! All the slave. Ten days or two weeks going. At the Pee Dee bridge we stop. Go in gentleman barn. Been there a week. Had to go and look for louse on we. Three hundred head of people been there. Couldn't pull we clothes off on that flat. Boat named Riprey. Woman confined on boat. She name the baby Riprey. The Mama named Sibby. Doctor come on boat. By name of Doctor Lane. White lady come to tend women. Get to Marlboro where they going. Put in wagon. Carry to the street. Major Drake plantation. One son Pat Drake. Wife a little bit of a woman.

I cook on that flat. Dirt bank up. Fire made on dirt. Big pot. Fry meat. At Pee Dee get off flat. Dirt camp to stay in. To hide from Yankee. Dirt piled up like a potato hill.

I so glad for freedom I fool. I sing "Freedom forever! / Freedom evermore! / Want to see the Devil run, / Let the Yankee fling a ball. / The Democrat will take the swamp!"

Master been hide. Been in swamp. Yankee officer come. "Where Mahams Ward and John J. Woodward?" Yankee come to tell them take these people out of the dirt camp. They put us in a flat and carry us back.

Put food and children in flat. We been walking. We see a man's house. Man say, "Come out. You steal my turnip." Stay in brush arbor when night come. Make camp way down the road somewhere. All squeezed in. We hit Bucksville and we meet a friend. Say, "People hungry." This the middle of the night. Snow on ground. That night I cook all night! Rice. Baked potato. Collard. Cook. Give a quilt over your head. I sleep. I sleep in the cotton. I rooted up in the cotton. December. Winter time. Cook all night. Corn bread, baked potato and collards. We get to Bucksport, people begin to hoop and holler.

It's the Democrats hiding in the swamp and Lincoln's Republicans who have freed the slaves, but in my own times it's been the Democrats who have taken up the struggle. In any event, I heard nothing in my childhood to suggest that slavery was a happy and normal way of life. While the members of my family deeply honored the effort made by our ancestors in the defense of "the Cause," Mama was careful to record events exactly as they were described to her. We don't have just the accounts of white Southerners to rely on.

Hagar Brown of Murrells Inlet. Whenever she entered a house, she raised her arms and said, "Lord, bless this house and keep the soul." Photograph by Bayard Wootten. North Carolina Collection, University of North Carolina Library at Chapel Hill.

Genevieve Chandler Peterkin and husband Bill Peterkin, ca. 1980.
Photograph by George Morgan.

Jim Peterkin and mother,
Genevieve Peterkin

Jim Peterkin, November 1971,
fourteen years old

Eason's Store, Murrells Inlet. Photograph by George Morgan.

A Light

ARRIVING AT FORT MOTTE IN the late 1950s was a shock. I couldn't believe the paternalism, the dependence. I suppose the difference between there and the Inlet was only one of degree, but on Lang Syne black families were still living in the cabins the slaves had occupied. Nothing had changed. Same plantation street and many of the same things happening on that street. In Murrells Inlet, at least, a small amount of money came in from work in the creek, the restaurants, and farming, and blacks had owned their own homes. And much later we tried to help those at Fort Motte do the same. When the chance came up my stepson, William, and I bought fifteen acres near Fort Motte and offered this at a reasonable price for home sites to those who wanted to own their own home, and some of the younger people did accept.

But I've got to back up. When my mother-in-law, Julia Peterkin, came to Lang Syne in 1903 she had to be nurse and social worker, and she wrote of one of her patients and told me of him too. An old black man, the foreman, was a diabetic, and she was in his cabin soaking his feet, just trying to bring him some relief. Instead of using Epsom salts she'd put mercurical something in the water which should have done the same thing. But then to her horror his toes just started to float to the top. They came off in the water. Obviously gangrene was the cause of this, but the foreman's family blamed her. Her father, Dr. Mood, had to come and amputate both legs. The foreman was a tall man. Julia used this incident in her novel *Black April* and didn't change much. When the foreman knew he was going to die, he said, "Miss Julia, be sure I be buried in a man sized casket. I'm 6'4" so bury me in a man sized casket."

Coming to that farm over fifty years later I experienced much the same. Not nearly so dramatic but certainly situations that required a trained nurse, which I was not. But from one such encounter I did make a significant leap in faith.

You almost start out pretending to be a Christian. I think most do and then we have a lot of true conversions along the way. I don't think anybody has a "big bang" and they're done. I guess my point is that I was really burdened. My husband's aunt, Aunt Laura, had come to us from California after Julia died. She had other family where she stayed at times, but now she was with us. A wonderful woman but eighty-seven years old, suffering from Parkinson's, and physically larger than I was. It took help to raise her from the chair. Jim was six. I'd get him up and send him off to school and then give Laura breakfast and help her dress, and that was how my day went.

At this point Mamie, the black woman who'd been Julia's cook for years, got diabetes and had to have a leg amputated. And her children lived in Jamaica. Jamaica, New York. She came home from the hospital, and no one had even explained how she must give herself insulin shots—which hardly mattered. She declared that she wasn't about to stick a needle in herself. That afternoon I had to rush to the Health Department and learn how to use a hypodermic needle. (You practice on an orange.) Then race to the drugstore for the medicine. The next morning I tended to Jim and then to Aunt Laura and then went out and gave Mamie her breakfast, dressed the amputation wound, and gave her the insulin shot. And at each stage of this process Mamie would say, "Thank you, Jesus." Breakfast—thank you, Jesus. Dressing—thank you, Jesus. Shot—thank you, Jesus.

This went on for about three weeks. Nothing but thank you, Jesus, and I guess I was just exhausted. That day when I was done I went out on her porch and said "God damn" out loud. I thought, "I come here every day and she never once says 'thank you, Sister.'" Then literally a light seemed to shine on me. A physical turn-away-the-dark light. And my poor dumb heart was enlightened. I realized at that moment that

God puts us where he needs us—or tries to anyway. I thought, "God uses us to do his work, so what was I complaining about? Mamie's a better Christian than I ever hope to be. She knows who to thank." Of course, Lillie had been no different. Nor were many other black men and women who had lived with deprivation and hardship but saw only God's work around them. "Jehovah, I depend on you." That's what Aunt Hagar said.

Mamie began to use a wheelchair and after lengthy practice with the orange learned to give herself the shot. And one of her daughters came not long after and helped to care for her.

And me? I'd seen the light. Or at least a sliver of the light. And taken a step along God's path. At least, a small step. I hope. And pray.

Civil Rights

I REMEMBER WHEN FRANKLIN ROOSEVELT died. I'd gone up to the store for a loaf of bread and people were just standing around. The atmosphere was so strange, and the storekeeper said, "Sister, the President's dead." I was almost grown but I ran home crying. When we were at Wachesaw, Daddy had bought a battery-operated radio, and though Mama and Daddy listened to the entertainment, their reason for owning a set was to hear President Roosevelt's fireside chats. I got much closer than that.

Sometime around 1944 Mama and I were driving to Georgetown and stopped because the drawbridge was open. Both sides were lined with soldiers, and a yacht was approaching. Mama called out to a soldier, "Young man, what are you all doing here?" He told her he had no idea. I jumped out of the car, and two of the soldiers made a space for me at the rail. Here came the yacht and there was no mistaking President Roosevelt. He was seated on the bow in a deck chair with his white Panama hat on and a cigarette in the long holder in his mouth. I got so excited I yelled as loud as I could, "Hello, President Roosevelt" and waved both hands. Someone helped him to his feet, and as the yacht passed through the bridge he took off his Panama hat and bowed to me. After that how could I be anything but a lifelong Democrat?

Of course, I was hardly alone. I read somewhere that he'd gotten 95 percent of the South Carolina vote in that last election, down from 98 percent the time before, and around Georgetown it's possible he got it all. The president was already ill by then and resting at the nearby home of his adviser Bernard Baruch, which I'm sure made him even more popular around Georgetown and the Waccamaw Neck.

But times change. Bill and I both stayed Democrats, but our friends would say something like, "You had better wake up and realize that if you're white you have to be Republican." Being white was hardly a reason to change my political affiliation—but that was what was happening in the 1960s. Of course, this all had to do with the integration of the schools. That's why the Confederate battle flag started flying over the capitol building in Columbia. People who remember 1962 know why that flag is up there. Hardly a secret. And that flag is still flying.

Well, my husband and I knew the Supreme Court certainly wasn't going to reverse its 1954 school decision, so the logical route was to integrate the public schools and end the Jim Crow laws. Not many around us agreed though, and soon civil rights organizers were coming into our county to register black voters. Our own black workers told us they were being visited, so I began to approach these young women and say, "When you're out on our farm come by and see Bill and me. We'd like to know you too." We started having them to lunch in our house. Interesting people. Most were from Indiana and Ohio. One was from New York state. I attended meetings when they were organizing something revolutionary called OEO, and at others we were discussing food stamps—all of which seems awfully innocent today. Still, this was not a popular course of action for a white woman in those days, and fortunately I was blessed with a husband, Bill, who felt as I did. At about this time I got a call asking me to serve as county chair to elect Robert McNair governor of South Carolina. And I agreed, but after hanging up I thought, "Oh, my Lord. I might hurt him more than help him, if people knew that Bill and I have lunch with civil rights workers." So I called back. I can't believe I was that paranoid, but I wouldn't discuss this over the phone. I drove to town and told the organizer who had asked me to serve that I could hurt the Democrats' chances. And he said, "Why do you think we need you?" So what we were doing wasn't a secret from the powers that be. And McNair won. That was in 1963. Actually, a couple years before that was when we had our eyes truly opened—but that incident happened in Murrells Inlet. We were on vacation and I drove out on the highway to go to the post office. In a field was this big cross totally tied up with straw. Before the sun had set everybody was talking about the coming KKK rally, and, of course, most of these people were the summer residents. Our son, Jim, was so small at that time that we'd try and put him in bed early. The older children would be outside still playing so we'd read to him. Bill was in the bedroom doing that. I went out on the back steps, and I could hear the rally very clearly because they were using loudspeakers.

What was so awful to me was that every man who spoke was introduced as "Mr. So and So, a minister of the Gospel." Of course, they'd just taken up preaching, the ones my mother called "yard ax preachers." They hadn't graduated from the Union Seminary or any other seminary. But still Mr. So and So and Mr. So and So would take off: "Men, if you love your wives and daughters, you will come up here and join us tonight. You will join if you love your wives and daughters—if you love your wives and daughters. Oh, yes, I have hogs at home. I feed my hogs but I don't eat and sleep with them. I got a dog at home. I feed my dog but I don't eat and sleep with him. I got a mule at home but I don't eat and sleep with him."

All of it, the most racist thing I'd ever heard, and I'd heard plenty. And worst of all, I was a quarter of a mile away but could hear perfectly, and I knew I had black friends who were within that quarter-mile radius too. And I remember sitting on the steps and thinking especially of a woman who had a little boy who was exactly my little boy's age and a girl just a shade older. I knew she was home hearing this and that if I was her I would want to take a shotgun, go there, and start shooting. In fact, my feelings were that strong anyway. I remember that an airplane passed over and I felt that if there was a God in Heaven he'd drop a bomb on that happening right now. My feelings were that strong. A lot of the summer people stood in the trees watching, and they were astonished that something like that could still happen. They said the cross must have been treated with oil because it went in a blaze. The next day the charred cross was still in that field beside the highway.

So strange and so ugly, what was said when the schools were integrated. Claims that the blacks were dirty and smelled bad. Lillie Knox was
the cleanest person I ever knew in my life. Her clothes were scrubbed
and starched, and she smelled perfectly wonderful. She smelled of bay
berries and cedar berries. I just couldn't understand these attitudes.

The really bad thing that happened, though, was much later, in
1968. Some students from the black college in nearby Orangeburg
wanted to go bowling. This is hard to believe today 'cause it all sounds
so crazy and senseless. But the bowling alley was whites only, and when
the black students protested, the state's highway patrol showed up. In
the confrontation that followed three students were killed. This was
known as the "Orangeburg Massacre."

I went down to Charleston to a women's church convention at St.
Luke's Cathedral, and Bishop Temple presided. I don't remember a
thing about his talk that day except that he ended by saying, "Ladies, go
back to where you live and if there's not some sort of bi-racial committee working in your community, you go home and organize one." I
went home and got in touch with the president of the NAACP, Hope
Williams. I knew him before that, but we weren't really acquainted.
And we did get to be friends. Occasionally I still get a message from
him. Oh, he was the most unlikely of people for me to be friends with.
But we started the group and, in truth, weren't very successful, at least
with attendance. The only whites who would meet with us were two
dear young Methodist ministers who had little country churches. I
don't even remember their names, but I did appreciate them so very
much. Every black minister in the county attended. We kept that group
going for a long time, and some serious confrontations were avoided
because we met. You see, I could at least contact the powers that be and
tell them what was being thought and said in the black community. We
made a difference at the time. But it was scary—very scary.

On the surface I can't say that my place in the white community
ever changed. I never felt any real rejection from them then or even
earlier, but if I hadn't been married to Bill and if his mother hadn't been

of local as well as national importance, I would have had a different experience. I know that's true. At one meeting I even said, "If I were married to someone else and living in a mobile home my reception in Fort Motte would be a hell of a lot different." It even helped that Bill was farming, growing soybeans that he could sell to whomever he wanted. I came out of one meeting, and a woman whispered that she wished she could speak up like I did but that her husband sold trucks to the county. No doubt I was insulated from the consequences of my actions. But that was just out in public. Plenty of anonymous threats were made.

The following year, 1969, we were getting ready for the tricentennial in South Carolina. Three hundred years since the first settlement, and I was asked to serve as county chair of the celebration. They gave us fifteen hundred dollars to put on a week-long big to-do, so we formed a committee. I assumed that the county's money should be spent on a celebration suitable to the whole town, the whole community, both black and white. However, the rest of the committee hadn't gotten that message at all. I held a public meeting at the courthouse to try and get everyone involved. Honestly, that was an evening when I was really praying. Except for the committee, no one showed up at the courthouse but the black leaders—the political leaders, the church leaders, even many of the schoolteachers. It was obvious that they expected and should have expected to be included in this celebration. And I was thinking, "My God, what can we do?"

One committee member stood and said we should plan a tour of houses and maybe some of our black friends would be willing to open their homes as well. This was meant to be a peace offering, but it sure wasn't going to work in Calhoun County back in the 1960s. The white home owners weren't exactly rich, but much of the black community lived in real poverty. I knew touring houses wasn't going to mend any fences, and suddenly the notion of spirituals popped into my mind.

That celebration lasted a week so a lot would go on, but our big event was to be on the last night out at the town's park, down at this beautiful lake. For months ahead of time I went every Sunday afternoon to different black churches and listened to their choirs. And those churches latched onto this idea. They were so happy to be included, and they would be performing music that was beyond the capabilities of most of the white citizens. They'd be contributing what the white community couldn't.

We decided to give each church two selections to sing, which they chose and turned in ahead of time to prevent duplication. I wasn't concerned about this program since I couldn't imagine a Christian hymn being controversial. Then lo and behold my friend Hope Williams of the NAACP, who was also deacon of his church, sent in "We Shall Overcome" as a selection. I got in the car and drove to his house. My mother was visiting, and she went along. When we got there he was in the yard chopping wood. I introduced my mother, and then I told him I'd come about the song selection. I said, "If you come to the park and sing 'We Shall Overcome,' it will be just like the whites getting up and singing 'Dixie' to you." He said that hadn't occurred to him. I said, "Whites only hear that song when it's on television with angry people shaking their fists." He said, "We sing it every Sunday in church, but you're right. I tell you what we'll do. We'll sing 'Let Jesus Fix It for You.' They both say the same thing, don't they?" Oh, he was a wise man and patient. And a true diplomat. Then he turned to Mama and added, "Mrs. Chandler, we'll dedicate that one to you."

This planning went on for months, and the concert was shaping up to be a big success. Barbecue was to be served, and the Boy Scouts were going to float three hundred candles out on the lake as the spirituals were being sung. And it did work out. A wonderful and beautiful evening just as planned. But in the weeks leading up to that night I got all these threatening phone calls that scared me to death. "Mrs. Peterkin, you have opened a can of worms that never should have been opened in this county." And "You are going to cause the biggest race riots South Carolina ever saw." And more. I was really frightened. Really frightened. It's hard to believe being that paranoid, but again I was afraid to use the

phone in my own house. All this over singing about God's love and Boy
Scouts floating candles on a lake. And I didn't know who to turn to, for
this was the one time in my life I kept a secret from my husband. If I
told, he'd pack me up and move me to another continent just to get me
out of danger. I didn't even trust the local sheriff. Maybe I could have
but I didn't. Finally I went to the chairman of the Democratic Party in
our Calhoun County and told him that I was very frightened but that
this program was going to go on. He told me not to worry another
minute. He got in touch with the state police agency SLED, and they
had plainclothesmen all over the park that night—whom nobody recognized as policemen. The program went perfectly. Every church choir
showed up and sang their songs. And the next morning the Orangeburg
newspaper had a giant headline—"CALHOUN COUNTY'S MOST
MEMORABLE NIGHT IN HISTORY."

Of course, by this time the schools were integrated, which should
have been a cause for Bill and me to rejoice but instead turned into
another heartache. Jim was approaching the fourth grade the summer
before integration, and at the supper table we would talk over things—
I guess we used the supper table to educate him. We discussed how the
tax system paid for the schools and so they belonged to everybody.
Therefore, if black children chose to come to his school it was theirs as
much as his. We wanted him to have the right attitude. We played hell
with that child.

Up through the third grade he loved school and loved his teachers.
But we had indoctrinated him. Early in the fourth grade I got a note
from the principal saying, "It is important that you teach Jim 'When in
Rome do as the Romans do.' We do not plan for this to work in our
school." They actually imagined that they could undermine integration
and make the poor little black children go back where they came from.
That was the attitude of some of the faculty.

I went to see Jim's teacher and discovered exactly what the principal's concerns were. At recess Jim picked black boys to be on the
kickball team. He played with them. She said, "We don't plan for that

to happen on our playground." I don't know what I should have done then. We couldn't very well untrain our son from being a decent human being. We did warn him that others didn't share our feelings or his and that would make it difficult for him. And it was difficult—so difficult that he was soon calling home, complaining of a stomachache. He'd leave fine in the morning, but soon he'd call. By the spring of the year I was carrying him straight from the school to the doctor's office. But they couldn't find anything wrong. I'd carry him home, get him a glass of milk, and he'd be fine. I'd never dealt with an ulcer. But Jim had an ulcer in the fourth grade.

I took him to a pediatrician, and that's what he found. He saw stress as the obvious cause and suggested that when Jim finished the school year he immediately go into the hospital. That was another couple of weeks. I was to tell the teacher what was happening and make her understand how important it was for Jim to finish the year with as little fuss as possible. We were going to let him coast with his grades and the rest. I did this. And so the first time Jim left the classroom for a piano lesson, she told the rest of the class that Jim Peterkin was very ill: "He has an ulcer in his stomach."

Well, one of our neighbors had cancer at that time, and she too was said to be "very ill." And some of those classmates knew this and assumed an ulcer and cancer were the same. That was the end of a stress-free finish to the school year. We took Jim out of school, and once he was in the hospital the doctor was wise enough to get the truth out of our son. Jim played with the black children, which caused some of the white children to reject him, and he couldn't deal with this. Thus the ulcer. We kept Jim on a strict diet that summer and he healed, but the doctor said he shouldn't go back to public school. So there were Bill and Sister Peterkin, the biggest liberals in the county, and the only alternative we had was to move our son into one of the all-white private schools that had been organized to fight integration. We kept him there until the eighth grade and then enrolled him in a boarding school. Our son had grown up playing with black children at Fort Motte. You work so hard for things to work out, and sometimes they don't. It's almost like you've been hit below the belt. But then the discrimination that this single white child experienced was being experienced by hundreds of thousands of black children. But this single white child was our Jim.

Doubts

I'D BE RIDING DOWN THE road with Bill and he'd see a dead dog on the side and say, "That dog is dead as Hector. That's the end." Well, I'd answer him, "Bill, I expect when you die, you'll be in for a rude awakening. By golly, you're going to wake up and find yourself in a better place." I know that sounds like hard teasing on his part, but back then in the 1960s I was always preaching to him—and at him. A friend, Charlotte, and I were going around, very religious, and our husbands were amazingly tolerant.

Still, Bill didn't go to church except Christmas Eve. His mother, Julia, had influenced him that way. She'd been raised by her grandparents, who were strict Methodists. In fact, her grandfather was a minister, a circuit rider who went by horseback among several churches. These two were very stern, and she was in rebellion against that and passed the message to the next two generations. But when she went into the Orangeburg hospital for the last time, a time that was so difficult for Bill, I went to see her and she said, "Sister, I thought I'd wake up with the angels this morning." I smiled, and she said, "What do you think will happen to me?" And then she spoke of her grandfather: "I've rejected all he taught me, and now I've had months to lie here and think and I've really come back to believe in exactly the things he said." She went on to say that she thought I was a much better Christian than she, for though she'd majored in religion and studied all the religions of the world, I understood in my heart. She said, "I just got tangled up with people who thought they were too intelligent to believe this simple message." She was talking about her New York crowd, other writers, the unbelievers.

Not long after that the doctor told us to take her home for a visit because this would be our last chance. We did that, and I gave her our bedroom because it was on the first floor. I'll never forget. We put her in the four-poster that Mama had given us when we got married, and Julia said, "I would hate any old woman who came in and took my bed." And yet my mother-in-law was a kind person. Only she was kind in a secretive way, giving money to all sorts of people and causes but never taking credit, and in the open where it showed being outspoken and blunt. And she was fearless when it came to standing up for people less fortunate than herself—black or poor or disadvantaged in any way, and I did try and learn this from her. So that time in the hospital when she told me she thought she'd wake up with the angels but what did I think would happen to her, I'd answered with the truth. I said, "I don't know, but whatever's good and whatever's perfect, that's where you'll be. I'm sure of that." I did feel that way about her.

Now, Mama had a much firmer vision of the hereafter, or at least presented one to us children. Perhaps this was because Daddy had died, for besides speaking of heaven, she would talk about him constantly to us—especially to my brothers, for they'd been very small when he went. She'd take us to the cemetery and we'd rake leaves in the family plot. She'd say, "Oh, I feel so close to Tom here." She made us under-stand that Daddy was somewhere and that he was overseeing, watch-ing—that he and God were up there keeping an eye on us, which was comforting, of course. And yet, for herself, Mama too had doubts about the hereafter and all the rest.

But I can't imagine that Lillie had doubts. She died at about the same time. Lillie didn't smoke, but in her mind that would constitute rest. She'd say, "Sis, when Lil's an old woman you going to come and bring me my pipe tobacco and I'll be sitting in my rocking chair." But it didn't happen that way at all. Lillie got cancer while we were living in Fort Motte. That first summer before Jim was born I didn't come down to the Inlet because pregnant women weren't supposed to take long car trips, but the next summer I brought Jim, and Lillie would sit and rock him. She'd just spend the day with us. I guess she could have been sick then and we didn't know it. By the next summer she was in bed. Mama and I arranged for a nurse to come to her house and give her shots of morphine. The last time I went to see her, I was sitting there trying to just sit and talk to her and she was in so much pain she didn't feel like company. She said, "Darlin', there's nothing you can do for old Lil anymore. You go on home and take care of your little boy."

I should have done more, but I don't know what. Lillie had her faith, which was so absolute I can't help but be envious. She was completely emotional when she entered into a church service. Jesus was someone very real to her, and that did influence me or at least pointed me in the right direction. Such warmth and certainty is to be envied, and even today I envy some of my black friends. Mamie, the black woman with diabetes who each time she was helped would say "Thank you, Jesus." I wasn't around to help Lillie, but I could help Mamie, and that did lead me to a great revelation. As I said, one day I just left her room and walked out onto the porch and started crying and thinking, "Damn, it's time to thank Sister." And I did realize at that moment it was the Good Lord making me tend to her and I wouldn't have done otherwise.

When you consider what blacks endured under slavery, it's amazing that they would even convert to Christianity. Sometimes the planters would encourage the founding of a church among them, but what could they have seen in the religion of their masters? I mean the parts of the Bible that dealt with the Israelites in captivity were denied them by the whites. And yet they took Christianity and made something grand.

Henry Small, who's almost 101, had a conversation with me just the other day, and I asked him about the visions he'd experienced during the course of his life. And he repeated them for me—visions that were like dreams, only he was very much awake. When he was a young man he'd been caught in a wildfire that raced through a part of the Freewoods. He climbed down into a ditch that was partly filled with water. He couldn't outrun the fire because the broom straw and pine needles were feeding the flames. He lay in the ditch and asked, "Lord, am I going to die?" And the Lord had answered, "Henry, you are going to die but not now." Then when World War I came he enlisted. This was a bit unusual for a black man in the South, but that was how he and several others acquired substantial land in the Freewoods—the military pay. Anyway, he was in the army and he was frightened, and with good reason because plenty of men were losing their lives. So he asked, "Lord, am I going to die?" And for a second time he heard the Lord speak very clearly, "Yes, Henry, but not now." So when I went to see him the other day, I ended up teasing him. He was in bed with his daughter and grandson around to take good care of him. I said, "As long as you're doing this well, the answer is still "Yes, Henry, but not now."

After all these years I'm still looking to my black friends for answers—for some notion of how to live this life and what to expect in the next one. It's strange. I mean it's safe to say I had a religious upbringing. On Sundays I'd go to the Belin Methodist Church and then the Presbyterian church for afternoon services. If the Baptist church had a revival, we attended. We learned the Presbyterian catechism. We didn't thread a needle on Sundays. Or play cards except when we snuck off to the neighbors. Then after leaving home I went to Coker College, which was started as a Baptist institution, and I usually attended the Baptist church up there. I joined the Episcopal church when I married Bill, and then after his death I started going to the Lutheran church with June. I've been the rounds, and I'm happy being a Lutheran. For one thing, we emphasize the belief in "saved by grace," which means your good works don't have a damned thing to do with anything. As a Methodist you had to be "good." Now I just have to have faith and believe in Christ. I was raised to believe that old drunk Mr. So and So down the road beats his wife and will never get to heaven. But maybe this sinner is nearer to salvation than we are, which is a generosity that seems to be a natural part of the black world.

But I suppose there's even more to it than that. All those years since the 1960s I read practically nothing but psychology and religion—the Swiss psychiatrist Paul Tournier's *A Place for You*. I read it more than once and gave copies to friends. But I read all these people so long ago I can't remember what they said. I suppose I have absorbed the lessons, but so many books, like the French writer Pierre Teilhard de Chardin's *Building the Earth,* were wonderful at the time, and now I'm on my own again. What's in heaven? Would they let dogs and flowers into heaven? My old friend Dr. Smith came by the other day, and we touched on the hereafter. He was going down the steps and stopped to tease me. He said, "I can't imagine singing hymns through all eternity. We're standing up there in church singing hymns and praying that Jesus will come tomorrow, or this afternoon would be better, and then we can sing those same hymns forever. You know we don't mean it."

Well, he's right. I mean, I love the music but what's a heaven without dogs and flowers?

When we were up at Fort Motte we had a new young Episcopal priest, Ralph Byrd. His first Sunday, and my stepgrandson Willy was eight and Jim was ten and both were up there singing in the choir stall. Our young priest was fresh from the seminary, and he was just preaching away and preaching away, and finally Willy came up like a jack-in-the-box, stood right up under the pulpit and said, "Mr. Byrd, I think you've talked long enough now." And Ralph Byrd said that was a valuable lesson, one of the best he'd been taught. I'm going to take it myself, but I'll return to the subject of flowers and dogs.

Fish Stories

BACK WHEN I WAS PROBABLY fourteen, fifteen at the most, I was invited to this birthday party. Actually, June was invited and they just let me tag along. It was going to be a moonlight cruise on the *Anne Howe,* the boat that old Captain Luther had built and which the whole community called the "Ark" when he was building her. That boat sat on the chocks forever, it seemed. Slow getting built, but she was handsomely done, and she was in Murrells Inlet until fairly recently. Captain Luther would take parties out, deep-sea fishing parties. Half-day trips mostly, so not too far offshore. All my brothers worked for him at one time or another as deck hands when they were growing up.

Now, at fourteen I'd been offshore fishing a good bit but didn't know a thing about running a boat—at least not from hands-on experience. But I had been with Luther on the *Anne Howe* a few times before and seen him run her. So—he took the birthday party out, but Captain Luther had a drinking problem. An evening trip like that one probably wasn't a good idea. Morning would have been better. We realized this somewhere well off of Garden City. He turned the wheel, and when he did, he eased right down on the deck and stayed there. I grabbed the wheel and had to keep it because nobody on the boat knew anything more than I knew. This was a cruise for sixteen-year-old girls.

It was still light, light enough to find the mouth of the inlet, anyway, but dark was closing fast. And we crossed the bar in the night. I hit bottom, but the *Anne Howe* slid over. Thank the Lord. And then heading down Main Creek, I wondered, "How will I get to the dock?" I had no idea how to stop the boat and secure her to the pilings. But within a few minutes Luther stood up. He just rose up. He grabbed the side of that boat and lifted himself and grabbed the wheel and brought her right in. He'd been utterly passed out. I know he wasn't faking—this was no elaborate practical joke, or he'd have come to fast when I bumped that bar.

So when I started fishing with my husband offshore, I wasn't a total novice at navigation. I did have that one trip with Luther under my belt. Oh, Bill loved to fish. It was his passion. He'd courted me fishing. That was in the eighteen-foot boat he'd built himself. When Jim was about twelve we got a bigger one, a twenty-four-foot fiberglass boat we called *The Second Honeymoon,* though that never got painted on the stern. Good flotation, fiberglass, like a Boston Whaler but built in Tarpon Springs, Florida. That's when we started venturing offshore. I'd run the boat and Bill would do the fishing, which worked well because I seemed to have some odd sense of where I was and always got us back home. We didn't have a Loran or any of that other electronic magic in those days. We had a compass. That's all. But if we left Murrells Inlet and went out at 3:30, went twenty or thirty miles and trolled half the day, I could still judge where we were. I could judge the wind and the tide and get us home.

We were trolling for king mackerel and Spanish mackerel but often caught dolphin and other fish too. For Spanish mackerel we had little metal spoons up on the surface, but for the kings a metal plate would carry the bait, a whole small fish, down deeper. That's when we'd get barracuda and dolphin too. This was the edge of the Gulf Stream, about twenty-eight to thirty miles off—where the water begins to change color. During the summer there'd be a dozen boats around us, which was pretty safe, but by late fall we'd be by ourselves. Pretty foolish, but Bill would have rather fished than eat, and occasionally we'd have friends along and we always had a citizens band radio on board. But my brother Tommy would say, "Sis, one day that boat's going to be found floating off the coast of Africa and yours and Bill's skeletons are going to be on it." He didn't like us off there, especially not in late fall.

One afternoon we had a young man from a local college with us, Frank. He'd never been offshore. We got out there, and Bill and Frank were catching king mackerel. But the days were getting shorter. I said, "We've got to head in." But they insisted on staying. Catching and catching. I knew we were twelve or more miles from the inlet and the sun was dropping. "Just circle one more time, Sister. Just circle one more time." Back then there was no limit on the king mackerel. Finally I said, "You all pull in your lines because we're going home." But I'd waited too long to say this. Before we reached the mouth of the inlet it was hard dark. This was long before the jetties were built or lighted markers went up. In the daytime you'd locate the water towers from Litchfield to Surfside and know the inlet was in between, and if you had to, during the summer months you could use the lit-up beach houses at night, but this was after the season—unlit houses for the most part.

In the dark I came up on a pier which could have been coming out from any one of three beaches, but I decided this was Garden City and headed south. Which was right, but still that inlet was awful to enter. The channel would change very quickly, almost from morning to evening, it seemed. The captains on the big boats just moved the buoys to accommodate the shifting way. We hit the bar a few times coming in that night. With each hit I'd hear the birds fly up off the bar as we scraped over. What guided me finally was a row of lights on the eave of Nance's Restaurant. I saw those and knew we were home.

I guess I could mention one other trip which also involved a young man. David was about seventeen and from Conway. We were about eighteen miles out that day, Bill and David fishing and me running the boat. We'd been idling because they'd caught a big dolphin and were getting him. A very big fish and so gorgeous. There's nothing more beautiful than a dolphin coming out of that green water near the Gulf Stream. Those streaks of gold and blue on the fish. Incredible. And then they're in the boat and that fades to gray so fast. This boat had a hardtop cabin and we were trying to calm the poor fish, but once aboard it had sailed into the air and hit the hardtop overhead. He killed himself pretty quick. Not that we'd have released him. We were planning to eat that fish, which is delicious and called a Mahi Mahi nowadays.

Anyway, I'd been idling the engine while they landed the dolphin and now moved the knob forward, and nothing happened. The boat didn't move. I told Bill. He looked over the stern and said, "My God, the propeller's gone." He thought he had a spare but didn't. Well, David turned green—literally changed color. He'd been fine all day but now became violently ill. Bill told me to radio for help. I started thinking, "Lord, where are we?" I called on the CB and luckily got a friend who was driving in his car on the highway. I told him to call my brother Tommy. The friend asked for our location. I told him about thirty miles out and whoever comes should set the course for 330 degrees, which hopefully would bring them pretty close. I said we'd hang some towels on the outriggers.

The Wild Turkey was the boat that came for us, and the young captain asked how on earth I'd known the course setting. He'd come straight to us. I really had no idea. Intuition. Thank God. Otherwise Tommy would have been right and we'd have ended up off the coast of Africa.

Oh, but Bill did love to fish and I did enjoy being at the wheel. Over the years we caught a few big yellowfin tuna. I'll tell you, sometimes fishing does break your heart. Especially with those yellowfin tuna. I can remember not wanting to bring them aboard because their mate or friend would be right there beside them. They'd come up with their hooked companion. It breaks your heart when you see that other fish down there in the water. Oh, what do we really know about fish? Nothing at all. Nothing that matters. Our neighbor Cam was with us one day. She actually caught the tuna, which took two hours to get to the boat. That was the biggest I ever saw, and another was beside it bumping against it. You can't just reach down and free a fish like that, and anyway, Cam was determined. She caught him all on her own except when the line burned the skin off her thumb. Bill held the rod long enough for her to put on a bandage. We'd made plans the night before, and then Bill had gone over in the morning dark and tapped on her window. She and Bill's cousin Mildred were good fun on the boat.

I should also say that on that time with Frank, the time when I had to find the inlet in the dark, our poor son, Jim, was out there in his little whaler. Twelve years old and he was just inside the mouth circling around. On his last circle he saw our lights coming. He was on his way to call the coast guard.

Oh, what fools we mortal parents be.

Troubles

I CAN HARDLY CLAIM TO be a stranger to alcoholism. Between the moonshine stills, the Prohibition rumrunning along the coast, and now the restaurants serving minibottles, liquor has never been in short supply around Murrells Inlet. In fact, it seems like when I was growing up practically every family had at least one adult male with a drinking problem. Just like practically every family had a younger son who, after seeing what alcohol had done to his older brother or brothers, wouldn't touch liquor.

Mama's brother Uncle Clark Willcox was the teetotaler in that family, and their older brother Dr. Dick was the alcoholic. Of course, Mama didn't drink alcohol, but it was assumed that a woman wouldn't, at least a Methodist woman. Poor Mama. She'd signed a temperance pledge on the streets of Marion when she was eight years old and couldn't betray that. Though, in fact, she did sip enough fine European wines overseas to know how attractive they were and that she was right to stay away from them. Even when she was old and in June's and my care she'd only accept the apricot brandy the doctor prescribed if it was mixed with harmless-appearing apricot juice. She didn't want to set a bad example for her grandchildren.

But that's not to imply that, even today, I think of alcoholics as "bad" people. In my experience they are often the most sensitive and most intelligent and caring and loving individuals around. Not always, of course, but we had doctors who drank, like Dr. Dick and Dr. Wardie Flagg, because they really had just seen too much of the world's sorrow. And the Murrells Inlet attitude accepted them that way—which I should really say, for better or worse, was the Southern attitude. When

I was stationed in Germany, I noticed that the Southern boys were much more likely to get drunk than the others. Maybe that has to do with the fact that up north and elsewhere you had bars that served drinks by the shot instead of down here in the South where brown bagging was the law and they went off to a store (or a bootlegger) for a whole bottle, or maybe the culture just allowed that kind of behavior.

My husband, Bill, was my best friend. We generally saw eye to eye on important issues. However, he always encouraged me to be exactly who I am, even if our ideas differed. I believe this freedom is the greatest gift we can give a spouse, a child, or a friend. Oh, my husband was a good, good man in so many ways. We loved each other, and his love for our son was so very strong. And yet he turned into an alcoholic right before my eyes. Our family doctor watched this happen too. Bill's mother had gone into the Orangeburg hospital, which was twenty-four miles away. She had nurses with her around the clock, but we would go to visit at least once a day and sometimes twice. Plus we told them to call us to come if her condition changed, and they called often. They'd say, "Mrs. Julia's not going to make it until morning." We'd get that call, and Bill would rush off to see his mother in what he always thought would be her last moments.

Finally, Bill couldn't take this lingering illness. If they called at three in the morning he had to have a drink of bourbon before he'd get in the car. He'd never done anything like that. He might have a drink or two before supper and that was it. But now he actually began to carry the bourbon bottle with him to the hospital.

Then four or five days before she did die, he leaned over to pick up the newspaper and couldn't straighten back up. He had a pinched sciatic nerve in his back, which no doubt was connected to his emotional struggle as well. He ended up in the hospital and missed his mother's funeral.

And when he got home from there Bill drank. He continued to drink heavily for another ten years—until he reached the point where he was having a drink of bourbon even before his morning coffee. And

I let him. When a person becomes addicted to alcohol to such a degree, there is often an "enabler," and I know I was guilty of this. Finally, when Bill went to the hospital with pneumonia the doctor extended his stay so that Bill came home sober. And the doctor also recommended that we send Jim off to school. Both Bill and I had been against that. Bill had been sent off to boarding school himself and knew the disadvantages of not growing up in your own community. I'd vowed he'd stay home, but at fourteen Jim was off to Christ School in North Carolina, and though Bill had found the strength to remain sober, Jim stayed away at school.

Now, I figured our son would be safe in this church school. But the next year he was fifteen and bringing classmates home with him to the Inlet. He'd say, "Mama, I brought him 'cause he has a problem I think you could help." Those boys had divorced parents and all sorts of troubles, and I would try and say and do something constructive. It never occurred to me that my own son had a problem. Still, the start of that second summer he was acting differently. Normally he was the sweetest, most gentle-spirited young person, and now he wasn't. He hadn't been home long when I said, "Jim, I want to talk to you." We went out on the porch and sat in the rocking chairs. I said, "Now, you are always telling me that you think this one or that one of your friends has a problem with drugs. What about you? Have you used any drugs?" He said, "Yes." Just like that he answered, and I said, "What?" He said, "Marijuana mostly, but I did try speed."

It turned out he had marijuana under the floor mat of my car. I'd just driven to Columbia that day. I couldn't believe he'd let me go off with an illegal drug in the car. He said, "What are you going to do?" And I said, "Feed it to the fish." We went and yanked it out of the car, and I walked out on the dock with him trotting behind saying, "Don't do that. Don't do that. It cost five dollars." I shook the marijuana out into the creek.

What can I say? For my generation marijuana and what it could lead to seemed even worse than drinking, and when you look at the cocaine and crack cocaine addiction that came along next, I think we were right.

Either way, after dealing with ten years of alcoholism this seemed like a true piece of cake, and the cure did take. But in honesty Jim had a very thorough follow-up. For several years I'd been seeing a good psychiatrist in Columbia, and he recommended that Jim visit an associate of his, Dr. Trogden. Which did turn out to be the right thing to do.

In South Carolina and all the South there's a suspicion of such doings—or was. But Jim went and continued to go, and shortly before he died he told me that he felt like Dr. Trogden was his "best friend." Jim said, "I'd never have been one of those kids that gets caught up in the drug culture and disappears in California. I know that wouldn't have happened. The thing Dr. Trogden has done is to help me understand my dad."

From the ages of four to fourteen Jim had known his father only as a heavy drinker. He wasn't a mean dad. He was a wonderful dad, but a child can't understand when a person is sweet and kind, loving and gentle in the morning and in the evening might have no time for you—no time for you at all. So reacting that way to the marijuana, which actually did scare the hell out of me, definitely worked out for the best.

As for my husband's drinking, I've thought long and hard about including that fact—about being "too" honest. But since I have included it, let me just repeat that Bill was a wonderful man in so many other ways. I had these strong women influencing me most of my life—Mama, Cousin Julia, Lillie, I could even add June—but the truth is, my husband, Bill, influenced me the most. I married him out of not just love but respect. I can actually remember thinking that if I would be lucky enough to have children, I would want them to be like him. He was remarkable. Honest. Integrity like you seldom find. He had a wonderful sense of humor. If I was out on a limb—maybe a bit too far out—he was right out on the next limb over. He was my helpmate and I was his.

One winter day, a bitter cold day with sleet starting, I was driving to Orangeburg and passed this old man wearing what looked like a World War I overcoat—not World War II but World War I. He had a beard and looked like the worst kind of old tramp. He was walking toward Fort Motte, and I thought, "Good Lord, if he's still on the road when I come back, I'll have to pick him up and I'll be scared to." Well, I didn't see him on the return trip—until right where I was turning off to go home, and ahead of him was nothing but an eight-mile stretch of swamp-lined highway.

I drove on to the house and told Bill there was an old man out on the road and that he'd have to go get him because it was sleeting. We could at least let him sleep in our barn tonight. I was having sweet potatoes and sausage that night and almost had supper lined up and ready to go. I said, "Tell him to have supper with us and we'll find a place for him to sleep." And you know, right away Bill got in the car and went.

It turned out the old tramp was a Polish American. His name was Alshoski. He said this to Bill: "Thank you very much and tell your wife I appreciate that she cared but I've lived like this since 1910." I guess you could say he was homeless before we'd heard of homeless. He told Bill that he went to Florida and stayed the worst of the winter down there and then went back north. He told Bill he had everything he needed. He had a bundle with him, and he said, "I've slept in the woods and I'll not be cold and the sleet won't bother me." He told Bill he had plenty of food in his little knapsack and he appreciated the offer but liked the way he lived and didn't need any help.

That's how I remember my husband. Rushing off to offer help to Mr. Alshoski, who had chosen a completely different life for himself. Bill didn't say, "Oh, Sister. Please. No." He got straight up out of his easy chair in that warm house and went out into the sleet. My husband was a good-hearted man, and we loved each other very much.

Julia Peterkin

I'M A BIT RELUCTANT TO speak of my mother-in-law, Julia Peterkin. But I want to include at least the following about this incredibly talented and courageous woman. This is a story she told me several times, and the occasion did mark a turning point in her life.

Julia had begun to do a little writing, not publishing but just struggling. She was very depressed and had a lot to be depressed about. Her husband Willie Peterkin and his brother Preston had inherited the part of the farm with the house, but this came with a colossal ninety-thousand-dollar mortgage and the responsibility to farm land for their widowed sisters and a sister-in-law. Back in 1910 that was probably the equivalent of a million dollars. Then Julia's brother-in-law Preston, whom she loved very much, died at the age of twenty-six, leaving the debt all on Julia's husband Willie.

Now, on top of this was an earlier and even graver tragedy. When the birth of my future husband, Bill, approached, Julia had traveled over to her father's, Dr. Julius Mood, the man my Mama held in such esteem. He delivered Bill, but this was a breech birth with a labor of thirty-one hours, so Dr. Mood had almost seen his daughter die right in front of him. He couldn't stand the thought of her risking another pregnancy and convinced her husband to let him remove Julia's ovaries while she was still unconscious—a sterilization that would also come to affect her hormonal balance and moods.

It's understandable that this left her furious for the rest of her life with all men, most especially Dr. Mood, Willie, and even her son, Bill. I can remember her saying to him, "Your birth took me through the valley of the shadow of death." He was in his fifties then. She was incredibly angry and suffered from severe depression, but once she could discipline herself I suppose this tragedy was also a source of her drive and talent, which is what the following concerns.

One day, while she was still a young woman and hoping somehow to be a writer, she was lying on her back in a patch of thick green clover with the blue sky of Lang Syne overhead. And feeling nothing but this deep dark pain. When suddenly this whole flock of little green and gold birds came down right beside her. They were Carolina parakeets, once found in the millions but very rare then and soon to be extinct. She had never seen one, but here was a flock, descending into the clover beside her. They stayed just a moment and lifted off. Such a glorious sight, a whirling of metallic green and gold, just rising straight up until they disappeared. She felt that was a turning point. She was determined to do something with her life. Maybe not write, but something.

And what she said to her own son about putting her through the valley of the shadow of death—I couldn't believe she'd say that to him. But she had such anger that she couldn't let go of, at least not for the older generations. But for the young ones coming up she had a much more open love—for her grandson William, for my son, Jim, who was named for her deceased brother-in-law James Preston Peterkin, and for her great-grands and host of nephews and nieces.

Courage

FOR MUCH OF THE TIME that Jim was growing up, Mama was living with us. She would visit all around among her children, but she was with us often at Fort Motte and the Inlet. And, of course, we lived with Bill's mother, Julia, when Jim was very small, and after her death her sister Aunt Laura came to stay. Aunt Laura and Mama would both be there at times and were great friends because they'd actually met when they were both living in New York. The house was always full, and one evening I remember my husband, Bill, just started laughing. We were sitting in the living room. Our son was twelve or so, and Bill laughed and said, "Do you realize this is the first time you and I and Jim have ever been alone in this house?"

That was actually true, but I can't say that either of us really minded, and the company had certainly added a lot to Jim's life. When he was in the sixth grade the teacher was concerned that though his grades were good, Jim wasn't performing up to his potential. At her suggestion we took him to the university for testing. When I brought him in one of the psychologists said, "Mrs. Peterkin, you have lunch somewhere and you can pick Jim up at five o'clock." He said, "This will be a fun day for him. He'll like the test and have a good time." I felt comfortable leaving Jim after hearing that, but when I returned to pick him up this doctor said, "Mrs. Peterkin, please come in my office. I want to talk to you." This sounded ominous. Well, they had checked our son out and said he scored above high school senior and even college freshman level. Still, he had to stay pretty much at his proper grade level. Even though he might be bored, he wasn't a genius. He just knew so much. That doctor said, "I am baffled." He said, "We gave Jim a word association test, and for the word *courage* he responded: 'Courage is the ability to endure pain and suffering for something you believe in.'" The doctor said, "Where on earth would a child learn that concept?"

I had to laugh. I'd heard Mama tell him that the night before. They'd been discussing Hannibal crossing the Alps. When Hannibal's men had crossed the Alps they had endured pain and suffering for something they believed in. Anyway, having those three old women as constant companions gave him a pretty good education, but he still had to stay in the sixth grade.

The other incident I recall from that period was a strange dream that Jim had. He was fourteen. He'd been hearing snatches of the musical *Jesus Christ Superstar* on the radio. He had to have that album, which would mean me driving him to Orangeburg, which I agreed to on the condition that he get all his homework done before the record went on the player. I'd heard some of the music myself and didn't really like what I heard, but our young minister thought it wonderful, so that made it okay. Maybe. We got the album, he did the homework, and put *Jesus Christ Superstar* on the player. A booklet gave all the words, so I grabbed that up and followed along really wanting to find fault but couldn't. Jim just thought the music wonderful. He listened to that record two more times that same night. The next morning at breakfast my son said, "Mama, I had the strangest dream last night. I dreamed that I was on a sailboat, but it wasn't like any kind of sailboat I ever saw before. It was like two sailboats running side by side. The sails were rainbow colored." Of course, we'd never seen a catamaran in those days, never heard of one, and certainly hadn't seen sails that were anything but white. He said, "There were some people on the boat with me but I didn't know who they were. They were people I didn't know." He said, "I was on water that looked like Murrells Inlet but it wasn't Murrells Inlet. It was some place I'd never been before." He said, "Suddenly the boat came near shore and I jumped off. And when I landed, there on the shore was a long table stretched out in front of me, and everything you could think of good to eat was on that table. On both sides of the table the chairs were all full, and those were the happiest looking people I've ever seen." He said, "Then I saw the king was at the head of the table."

I interrupted him for the first and last time. I said, "The king?" He said, "Yes." I said, "How did you know he was the king?" He said, "He had a crown on his head." And I said, "Jim, I believe a dream about a king would be a dream about Christ." And Jim said, "Mama, I knew it was Jesus the minute I saw his face." Then he said, "I saw that the chair at the foot of the table was empty, and I knew that was my place. As I sat down, the only thing I wondered about was why the people who were on the boat with me didn't come too because the land I had come to was so much more beautiful than the land I'd left."

He was finished, so I said, "I don't understand—for some reason neither you nor I can comprehend you've been given a glimpse of what it's like to go from this life to the next."

In the years since I've thought about that dream about a million times. I don't believe in predestination—not one iota. I don't believe that someone is born to die in a certain way at a certain time—not your child or anybody else's. June's husband Ken had died in 1971, just a couple years before Jim had this dream. Ken had died young and he'd died suddenly. Someone gave June a book called *The Will of God* by Leslie Weatherhead— a small book with a simple message. The perfect will of God cannot be confused with circumstances of the instant. If you're at the wrong place at the wrong time—if your child walked down the road at the wrong time the truck would strike him, or the tide has risen an extra inch so he can't sail under that sagging power line. Well, God could intervene and change these circumstances, but we've got free will and He doesn't jump in. His concern is for a larger perfection. And in the same vein, there can be no predestination, for time has nothing to do with God and His purpose. Our time and our clock and calendar don't have a blessed thing to do with God. I suppose Jim's dream more than anything else has caused me to ponder this. After that dream he lived another six years. As a young boy on the farm

he'd attended black funerals, and he'd heard those preachers speak of
the "welcome table." They'd say, "Oh, he's sitting at the welcome table
today." That's not something we hear too much about in our white
churches, but the Lutheran liturgy does contain the phrase "and give us
a foretaste of the feast to come." That's in the Communion service. Jim
wouldn't have heard that, though. What he'd heard was "He's sitting at
the welcome table today. He's with Jesus." So in the end, I guess, that's
what that incredible dream really meant.

MODERN TIMES

Buck

THREE YEARS AGO I GAVE my dog Buck to the actor Jim Nabors. Buck was a German shepherd with a pedigree a mile long. And before him I'd had another shepherd, a smaller white female who was much easier to handle. That first dog was terrified of lightning, and the vet said she'd probably gotten that from me. But during lightning storms we children would go out with Mama onto the porch at the Hermitage. There was that porch roof over our heads, and she explained to us that her own grandfather would walk up and down their porch in storms saying, "The Heavens declare the glory of God and the firmament his handiwork." He caused her not to be afraid of storms, so she was determined we wouldn't be afraid of storms. So I know I didn't teach that first shepherd to be afraid either. But one day a storm came up and I wasn't home. She got so frightened she jumped the fence, and that was that.

June and I were visiting friends in Florida, and I was offered a puppy from next door in Alabama—a beautiful male shepherd whose father had actually come from Germany and cost twenty thousand dollars. I did think twice but then said yes, and here was this incredibly beautiful puppy going home with me. And he soon grew tremendous and, at least for me, completely unmanageable. I took him to obedience school for four months, and at the end of that time the woman trainer said, "Buck has passed but you have failed. He's matured around you, and he senses a lack of assurance in your voice." So that was that, but along the way she did recommend that I attend a dog show at the Myrtle Beach convention center so I would understand how truly beautiful Buck was compared to other shepherds. I went, and he was much more handsome than any of those dogs.

Still, if I had him on the leash and said "Heel," he just kept going and would pull me down and along so that my nose was plowing a furrow in the sand or even the pavement. My brother Bill said, "You have to find that dog another home. If you don't, you're going to spend your old age in a wheelchair." Bill kept harping, and lo and behold I got invited to a wedding in Tennessee.

I am not a total stranger to celebrity. One time the actor Robert Redford came to my house in search of Mickey Spillane. I believe they were making the movie *Butch Cassidy and the Sundance Kid* back then, and Mickey was one of the scriptwriters. This mile-long white Thunderbird pulled up in the yard, and this very handsome man dressed all in white got out, and I remember thinking, "That's Mr. Clean," off the household detergent bottle by that name. He was very polite and got the directions and went, and it wasn't until the next day at the restaurant that I discovered who I'd met. Of course, the waitresses couldn't forgive me for not recognizing Robert Redford, but I hardly ever go to movies.

I hardly ever watch television either, but I did recognize Jim Nabors. For years he played the lovable mountaineer Gomer Pyle on the *Andy Griffith Show,* and then I believe he was a marine PFC in a program of his own. I had at least seen him before, and he was just as delightful and friendly in person as on the screen. I was invited to the wedding of a young friend in Tennessee, a quite large and festive wedding that went on for about a week, and each night Jim Nabors was my dinner partner. He was recovering from an illness that had almost taken him, but he looked well then and I told him so.

Jim said, "Oh, the surgery, Sister, that wasn't so bad. What nearly killed me was that they had to come in when I was in Intensive Care and tell me my dog was dead." I said, "Well, of course, you've gotten another dog." And he said, "Oh, no!" Quite dramatic. "I could never love another dog like I loved her." His dog had been a big old Newfoundland, one of those very large breeds. I said, "Jim, you've made a terrible mistake. I've lived long enough to learn, and I know you have. If you lose a pet, you can go buy another one. If you lose someone you love, then you're just lost. But you can buy another pet, and before you know what's happened you love that pet as much as you loved the first one." I said, "I've learned that the minute something happens to my dog, I've got to get another one immediately. You've made a terrible mistake, and I have just the right dog for you."

And he said, "What are you talking about?"

I said, "I have a beautiful German shepherd, and I want to give him to you."

He declined. But since we were seeing each other every evening I could add something—sweeten the pot. "Buck was born in Alabama and so were you. Buck was meant to be your dog." But he would say, "No, Sister, I could never love another dog. I don't want your dog." And I'd say, "But I've got to find him a good home, and I know with you he'd be taken care of." But Jim still said no.

Then on the last day at lunch before the wedding I succeeded. I don't know why I hadn't thought of it before then, but I had managed to teach Buck one trick, a trick that I used to tease my friend Doris, who'd moved here from Long Island. I'd say, "Buck, would you rather be a Yankee or a dead dog?" and he'd roll on his back and stick his feet in the air. Buck was very smart. I could teach him that but not to stop chasing every squirrel that crossed his path. I explained Buck's one trick to Jim Nabors, and he said, "Oh, Sister, why didn't you tell me that before?"

So Buck had a new home. When I got back to South Carolina we put Buck on a plane to Montana. Jim lives on a ranch there. That really hurt, far more than I thought it would. I'd dealt with dogs dying, and after a while they were gone and that was that. But the fact that Buck was still living out there hurt me so badly. The day he flew to Montana I called and left a message on the answering machine saying I just wanted to make sure Buck had arrived safely. Jim called back in a little while, missed me, and left a message on my machine. He said, "I just have to tell you, your son knows his mother's voice. As soon as he got here I took him for a walk, and except for being tired he was fine. But when we came in the house I turned on the answering machine and he heard your voice. He's been sitting on the floor looking at that machine ever since."

Hearing that, I just started crying. His new owner told me I could visit, but I just couldn't go through separating again. This spring it'll be three years. For the first year I missed him so, even though I already had little Benjy, who is much more manageable and who I do love dearly. In fact, June teases me in a gentle way. We'll be sitting there and she'll say, "Do you know what you've done? You've just called Benjy 'my Jim.'" Oh, that's not so strange to call him by my son's name.

And Buck—I'm told that his new owner's ranch house makes Tara look like a cabin in the woods. And Jim Nabors also has a plantation in Hawaii where he raises macadamia nuts. Buck spends his winters there. Not bad for a Southern dog with just one trick.

Skin

My skipping of the third grade to go off with Mama and collect folk-lore finally paid off in a very surprising way. That was in 1937, the year I supposedly had rheumatic fever and would ride with her and listen to the stories being told in the black community. Almost a half century later, 1986 I believe, the historian Charles Joyner and I were working at the Waccamaw Middle School as volunteers. The teachers there had gotten a grant to put on a year-long folklore project—the purpose being to incorporate black history and folklore into the curriculum and show the contributions made by the blacks who came to this area as slaves. Black children would come away with a sense of pride in their past, and the white children would see that black people had done their share and more to settle the coast of South Carolina.

Charles was helping because he was a historian with an award-win-ning and popular book already published on the subject, and I was help-ing because I was a member of the school board. But one day Charles said, "Sister, you need to come to the school and tell some of those sto-ries your mother collected." I told him I didn't know them, and he said, "Oh, I know you do, and you'd remember if you tried." I didn't believe him. As long as my son was small, Mama was alive and telling those sto-ries to her grandchildren, so there'd been no reason for me to remem-ber them earlier. And yet, with Charles egging me on, it was amazing how all those tales came back. For eight years I went to the schools in Georgetown County telling them to the children—from kindergarten through the eighth grade and even high school on occasion.

Some of the stories were of the supernatural and superstitions—stories of the plateye and the hag and stories like the ones Uncle Remus had told, animal stories like those Joel Chandler Harris had collected in Georgia. Of course, there were minor variations between Georgia and here, but all these had come from Africa originally—and been slightly modified by an oral tradition of which I was unwittingly a part. Of course, I hadn't actually had to leave the house with Mama to hear many of these, for we had some of the very best storytellers coming under our roof practically every day. Richard Knox, Lillie's husband, would come to pick her up each evening, and sitting in the kitchen, he'd give these wonderful accounts of talking animals and the scary ones as well. And his brother Zacky Knox was another excellent source. In truth, as much as I loved Lil and as good a storier as she was, the men in that family were the best storytellers, and I expect that was true of other black families. At the day's end the wife would still have chores to do and it fell to the husband to settle the children down, and in those days before television and even radio a story is what settled them.

That said, I should also explain about hags and plateyes and the rest. A ghost is a spirit like Alice Flagg at the Hermitage. But a hag and a plateye are something else again. The plateye, at least in Mama's records, was always an animal-type critter and was usually a very harmless little critter like a squirrel or a house cat. And this animal would get your attention for the purpose of luring you into the woods and getting you lost. The plateye always has two big red eyes as big as dinner plates— he's the "plate" eye. Two red eyes as big as dinner plates, and of course, today people would say they're nothing but apparitions caused by swamp gas, those jack-o'-lanterns that float up out of the rotting vegetation, and that's probably true because the plateye stories I remember were always popping up in Mission Swamp, just inland of the Inlet. Here's a slightly altered plateye tale that I would recite for the children. The Gullah's been streamlined to the point where the student and the modern reader can handle it. The original teller was Addie Knox, who was a wonderful person and told this to my mother standing in our front yard. The day before she'd gone clamming, and returning home late in the evening this is what happened:

I scratch around and fill my bucket with clam. I come out the creek and it just getting on late in the evening. Not twilight yet but late. Captain Bill Oliver, he sitting there in his rocking chair on the porch of the Lodge and he holler to me and say, "Addie, whatcha got in your bucket?" I say, "Clam, Captain suh." He say, "You want to sell some of your clams?" and I say "Yessah. Don't want to sell all. I sell some." I go up on the porch and dug him out half my clam in his bucket and he give me a quarter for the half peck of clam and I take the rest of the clam in the bucket and head home. I going fix my children some supper. I come down de path right there by the old Belin Church cemetery and you now how dem live oak tree hang over that road. The moss trail right down to the path, right to the side of the road. Narrow little path. Just a little foot path there by the cemetery. I come to that path and I see a little house cat right there in that path in front of me.

I take my clam rake and I nudge that cat and I say, "Kitney get out the way." I touch that cat with that clam rake and you know what happen? That cat change right there in front of my eye. He change into a panther cat. Panther cat as big as a yearling bull. That panther cat got two big red eyes big as plates. Big as dinner plate and he keep looking at me and the tail up in the air just a twitching in the air. The hair all bristle on the back. I think, "Oh, Jesus have mercy on my soul. How I gwine get by that cat tonight? How I gwine get by that critter and get home to my chillen?" I put my bucket down and rear back with that clam rake and I come down on that cat back with that clam rake. You know what happened then? He change right in front of my eye. I hit that cat on the back with dat clam rake and he change—and he change into a twelve-foot alligator. That gater so big he tail off in the woods on one side the path and he head off on the other. He got them big red eyes big as dinner plates and just a looking at me. I think, "God have mercy on me. If I get to my chillen tonight I got to jump that gater back. If I touch that critter with this clam rake he going to change into something worser than a twelve-foot alligator so I gwine jump that gator back." I grab my bucket and

I grab my rake and I back up and I gets me a running start and I jump right over that gater. Don't touch em. If I touch em, he gwine be something worser. Then I run. I run the five mile home.

And Miss Genny, when I get to home, I fix them children some stew with them clam to go on the rice and before sunup, I out the bed and you know what I done? I walk all deh way to the Freewoods and I find Uncle Murphy and I tell him what happen to me last evening on the way home from the creek. I tell him about that plateye been in my path. He say, "Addie, I fix you something." He take a piece of calico and he take some gunpowder and sulfur and he mix 'em. He tie some knot on each corner of that little calico and give it to me with a safety pin. He say, "Addie, you carry this in your pocket or pin em inside your neck if you don't have pocket in your dress. You keep this on your body. The plateye can't stand the smell of gunpowder and sulfur."

Standing there in our yard, Addie Knox showed us that charm pinned in the dress right up by her neck. She certainly believed every word of the story I've just recited, and as a child I believed every word of it too. We grew up hearing all these stories just like the black children did, and we didn't stop believing them until we grew up. And of course, we had the supernatural much closer to us than Mission Swamp because I was sleeping in a bedroom called "The Ghost Chamber" and sharing the house with the ghost of Alice Flagg. And I expect I do still believe in Alice just a little bit because, unlike Addie's plateye, I'd seen Alice with my own eyes.

Now as I've already explained, Alice was a ghost and the plateye was an animal changling that leads you astray. But a hag was altogether another kettle of fish. A hag was always a woman. I would hear the modern-day children saying a hag was a man, but she has to be a woman because curiosity is what changes her and woman is always the curious one—or so they say. I used to hear what follows from both Lil and her husband Richard. Right now, even when we're all in our sixties or older, if you were to put the Chandler children in the dark and say, "Skin, skin, skin, you know me?" it would scare us to death. Lil and

Richard would tell this story in the kitchen with the old wood stove as the only light in that dark room. No lamp, just a bit of light creeping out of the firebox. They'd have us scared to death. They'd say:

There were two friends, Bubba and John, and they'd been down to the creek to oyster on the low tide. Late in the afternoon and on low tide. They're talking and Bubba said to his friend John, "John, I going marry next week." And John say, "You is? Who you going to marry?" Bubba says, "I going to marry Mary." John says, "You mean Mary, that Mary to the Freewoods?" "Yeah, that's the one." "Well, man you the lucky fellow. That a good looking woman."

So these two went on to their homes with their buckets of oysters and about a month later they're back in the creek oystering late in the afternoon. John says to his friend Bubba, "Man, how you doing with your new wife? Bubba say, "Man, there's trouble to my house. There is something wrong to my house. Every night God send, I go to bed and along about midnight I hear my wife get off the bed and go out and she shut the door and I hear the front door open and shut and she gone. I ain't hear nothing 'til just about sunup and I hear the front door open and shut and she back in the house and back in the bed." John says, "Man, you is married to a hag."

Bubba say, "What you mean?" John say, "Well, if she slip out about midnight and she gone 'til just fore sunup, she is a hag." Bubba says, "What I gwine do?" "This what you do," John tells him. "You listen tonight 'til you hear the bedroom door shut and then you hear the front door shut and wait 'til you hear the gate shut and you know she's out of the yard. Then you go to the kitchen and you get you the box of salt and pepper and go out there to the front steps and the hag always ball up her skin cause, you see, the hag come out of she skin when she gwine hagging at night. She gwine ball up she skin and leave 'em under the front step. You reach under the step and you gwine find that skin and you spread that thing out on the front porch there with the raw side up and you salt and pepper that just like you salt and pepper a piece of fish you gwine fry. Then you bundle that skin back up and stick 'em back under the step."

That night Bubba listened and sure enough she got out the bed, shut the bedroom door and then shut the front door and then when he hear the gate shut, he crawl off the bed. He gets the box of salt and pepper and he go and just like John tell him, that skin all up under the step. He put that thing out with the raw side up and he salt and pepper 'em and ball 'em back up and stick 'em back under the step. Then he go back to bed.

Just before sun up, he hear something sound like a screech owl out there in de front yard. "Skin. Skin. Skin, you know me. It's me." But skin ain't gwine let her in cause skin been salt and peppered. Skin ain't going let her back in. Bubba listen to that thing and he think, "Oh, God have mercy on my soul." That voice sound like a screech owl and then he hear the front door shut and she come in the door and he think she ain't back in she skin and she coming right back here. She opened the bedroom door and he stick his head up under the sheet and she snatch that sheet up off him and she wrap up in that sheet. She wrap up in that sheet from head to toe.

He say, "Mary, Mary, the sun coming up. You going get me some breakfast?" She say, "No, no, I sick. I too sick." "Well," John says, "You want me to walk out to the Freewoods and find Uncle Murphy?" Uncle Murphy been the root doctor. "You wants me to go find Uncle Murphy?" She say, "Uncle Murphy can't help me. I too sick. I too sick." He say, "Well, I guess I got to go to work." Poor Bubba, he get out of that bed and he get out of that room and he don't stop 'til he find his friend John. He say, "John, everything happen just like you tell me. Every thing happen just like you say. My God, she wrap up in the sheet and she ain't got no hide. No hide on she body. The skin ball up on the porch. What I gwine do now?" John say, "They ain't but one thing to do now. You has to boil her in oil." And that's what they done. They boil the hag.

Now that was a story about curiosity. Actually, it's a story about marriage too, but let's concentrate on the curiosity. The hag is a woman, and a woman is curious. I suppose I should have explained this first, but when she leaves her own house she's coming to yours, and if she can get inside she's going to jump on your chest and suck your breath right out of your nose. She does this while you're sleeping. Of course, what's being described is a nightmare. I had those kind when I was a child. I'd believe I was awake, but I couldn't move. I can remember wanting to scream for Mama. I couldn't move my little finger or make a sound. I was sound asleep in a horrible dream. And that's what I've always assumed a hag was—a paralyzing nightmare.

But the curiosity is another matter. Once she's out of her skin and she comes to your front door, she'll come through the keyhole. She's invisible once she's out of the skin. Nobody can see her, and she slips through the keyhole. What you have to do is have a sifter, the kind with the wire screen you sift baking flour through, and you hang that on the doorknob on the inside of the door. When the hag comes through the keyhole, she sees that wire and starts to count the holes. She has to count them because she's curious, and since there are so many holes in wire she's going to be counting the rest of the night. Once the sun is coming up, she's got to get back to her hide and you're safe. If you don't have a sifter, lean a broom against the foot of your bed. She'll see the broom and start counting the broom straw, and that keeps her busy for the rest of the night.

And there were other preventive measures, as well. A sewing needle dropped in a glass of water would keep the hag away from your bed. And there's a plant with little red spikes called "Gate Minder" by those interested in keeping the hag out of the house. And, of course, the most familiar protection was to have the window frame and door painted blue. It had to be a certain shade, a sort of light indigo. You'd see it on practically every house from here to Charleston but very rarely now.

But the celebration of such traditions as blue paint and even the stories I've just told you aren't always accepted today in a positive light. Starting back in the 1930s there was a backlash against the "local color" writers like my mother-in-law, Julia Peterkin. I mentioned this earlier when talking about the WPA records and my mother's short stories. No matter how lovingly the portrayal of Southern black life was, depictions of the "Gullah" culture were considered reactionary and degrading.

That changed in more recent years, and at least some effort is being made to once more celebrate this rich heritage. And I wasn't pulling any punches. I'd begin each lecture with an indictment of slavery. I would explain how it must have felt to be an innocent child playing in an African savannah and be snatched up and put in the putrid hold of a slave ship by white devils who you thought might be planning to eat you. And then end up in America without the benefit of family or any other references to your previous culture. But against all odds, the enslaved blacks had made a world for themselves here that was rich in music, worship, and storytelling. I was including all this, but what I couldn't change was the very obvious fact that I was white.

Along about this same time I tried lecturing to senior citizens too, but this proved to be much more difficult than children. These "Gullah seminars" were presented for retirees and vacationers from outside of the South and would each last five days. And always there were some black couples in the room, and always some of them were offended by the fact that a white woman was teaching them. And they let me know it. But I would go on and do my best, gradually they'd warm to the presentation, and on the last day they'd come up and say something like "I just wish I'd brought a tape recorder." But to reach that fifth and last day was such an emotional ordeal, I abandoned the lectures after the third try.

I even got gently criticized for being white and going to the schools to lecture on the black experience. And this did hurt but I can't say it made me stop, and I certainly had no regrets.

The very first time I lectured I had an eighth-grade class. I happened to say, "I just wish Zacky Knox could be here to tell you the story the way he told it to me when I was your age." Well, the next period was lunch, and since I was on the school board I often had lunch with the children anyway. Before I left the room this little boy said, "Mrs. Peterkin. Mrs. Peterkin can you have lunch with us?" I told him I'd like that and to save me a seat in the cafeteria. I spoke with some teachers and then entered the cafeteria, and here was a round table full of black children waving me to the place they'd saved. So I got my tray and sat down and said, "Now, tell me your names."

My main host said, "Darien Knox." And every other child present was descended from a Sandy Island, Freewoods, or Inlet family that Mama had interviewed. Darien Knox said, "Mrs. Peterkin, how did you know my granddaddy Zacky?" I told him that every story I'd told that day had been told to me and my mother by one of their grandparents. And then I just started to cry. I did feel like I was doing something worthwhile, and I stayed on that project until it just became more hours than I could handle. Anyway, by then the schools had "Sister Peterkin" on all kinds of tapes and cassettes.

Zacky Knox

ZACKY KNOX HAD A WONDERFUL sense of humor. He was a fine-looking man. His widow, Evelena, is still living and I do go to see her on occasion. Her daughter Drew takes good care of her. Evelena and Zacky had a lot of children, and Zacky was always worried about feeding them. He was working for my grandfather Clark Willcox when the old man was living alone at the Hermitage. Later when Grandpapa needed closer care we moved in with him, but at the beginning he just had Zacky doing everything—keeping firewood in the house and some gardening and anything else. Grandpapa would sell cabbage plants in the *Market Bulletin,* that sort of thing. I believe he'd started out paying Zacky and his friend five cents a day when they were young boys. That sounds terrible, but if Grandpapa could get by with paying a nickel a day I'm sure he did it. Zacky had a joke about his employer: "Mr. Clark, if you try and borrow money, he puts his hand in his pocket and reaches all around. Then he pulls out his hand and says, 'I ain't got a cent in the world.' He can say that cause he's named that pocket 'the world.'"

That was Zacky's view of Grandpapa, and when he was through at the Hermitage he'd come by our house and cut the wood for Lillie's cookstove. He was in and out all the time, and being still in his twenties, he didn't have to be as serious as Lillie and her husband Richard. Zacky could tease us and make us laugh. Here's an account he gave my mother—an account in his own words—of what it was like to deal with his sister-in-law Lillie.

Zacky Knox (Age Twenty-eight)

Here I was headed down to the creek to scratch a few clams. It was fixing to freeze up. A cold drizzle was a falling. Christmas was coming and I was in a tight spot. It was root hog or die. And I was planning on scratching a mess of clam for Lina and them children. They ain't going be on starvation long as I can handle a clam rake. Anybody is welcome to clam. Cold hand and wet foots is all clam cost anybody here on us creek. And I was making ninety and wondering if I was going to catch the tide. Trying to make it to the creek before them mud flat and oyster rocks cover.

Now Lillie know I got no regular job. She knows rations scarce for them seven head of children and she know I stay hungry. And here she fall on me! You see one them fishawk falling out the sky on one them mullet fish? That just how Lillie hit me. Here I passing her house and I hear somebody calling. I look and there Lillie head stick out the kitchen door.

"Zack! Oh, Zack! Ain't you want a hot cup of coffee?"

Now I never could refuse nobody nothing so I gone on in the kitchen out the cold. And that coffee not barefoot. Lillie have the cow cream and the sugar full. And when that hot coffee done drink and I just getting stimulated, before I can say "Thank you, Mam!" here Lil start.

"Zack, if I plant you, will you grow? Don't have to grow tall!"

By that she mean she going to ask me to do a little job. But I knows Lil. Lil sure tricky. I know what she going to say before she outs with it.

"Zack, before you go boy, how about taking two little planks and fixing a little pen for us little pig Abe? Won't have to board up but one side and two end. You can make it side the tool-house for one side. And, us'll help, Zacky."

That little pig Abe been brought there in a hat-box. He done spent one night in the kitchen. But they can't keep him in the kitchen. Got to have a pen. One thing always calling another.

And Lil, she have me hemmed in! I can't say "I ain't got time" because I didn't say "I ain't got time" when she said "hot cup of coffee." So I stand there rubbing my hands and turning and a thawing out by the stove. Can't seem to make up my mind to left that hot stove. And Lil go on.

"Zack, it ain't going to take you long. Just two little planks. Abe so little. Poor little fellow just a shivering. Took away from his Mammy before he wean good. Just able to suck down a little mush and soup. Poor little thing. He'll freeze out there by himself if us don't fix him up a nice warm pen and fill it full of pine straw for him to snuzzle down in. If he ain't fix nice and warm I'll meet him stiff dead when I come here tomorrow morning. That'd sure ruin my Christmas. Zacky, us can't let the poor little fellow freeze to death."

Lord, Lil can talk. She tricky. Nothing Lil won't do. I drink my hot cup of coffee and I make Abe's pen. All I can do. Then, the next day I got to run through that creek scratching clam and make up the lost.

Now all that happen last December. Here December come round again and Christmas in sight. Every potato eat out the hill. Eat up. One old Grandfather rooster leave on the yard. Not getting an egg. No meal. Corn gone—and you can promise your back but you can't promise your stomach. Little Evie foots on the ground. Her shoe sole gone. And Junior's saying he just got to have thirty-five cents reading book or he'll get whipped at school. And every day it's "Pap, I ain't got no tablet" or "I can't go to school without a pencil." Every day something or another. And Big Evie asking me "What am I going boil for them children's dinner?" So I just sold out. Had to get away from all them hungry eye staring me in the face. That place too hot. I'd rather go in the cold creek. So here I been heading down to the salt creek so I can get a few bushel of oyster. The man don't pay but fifteen cents a peck, but fifteen cent been a nickel and a dime. And what he don't buy, us can eat.

But that been a raw day. Sneaking cold. The north wind will freeze the marrow in you bone. Little cold rain hit you in the face like sleet.

So cold I got on all my clothes. Got on all two pair of my creek pants. I'm hoping the hole in the bottom pair will be cover up by the good place in the top pair. The same way with sweaters. All three so full with moth holes I have to put all three on one time. My boots do look good as new. Big old hip boot. Not a hole in the top part of them boot. Them would be good boot if it wasn't for the sole. Water slushing in them and every step I take water spurts up like an artesian well. But if they hadn't gone to leaking the Captain wouldn't have given them to me. So I has to be glad they does leak. Leaking boots better than no boots at all.

So here I was planning on going in the creek. Rushing along to catch low tide. Got to make it for young flood. When she once turn don't take no time for that tide to cover them oyster rocks. I was thinking if I just hit the tide right I'd get five bushels, and if I hustle maybe I'd get six. And a peck means fifteen cent. While I planning how much fifteen cent I going to make on them rock and how much meat and meal I going buy to full up them children for Christmas, I find myself by Lillie house and somebody hail.

"Zack! Oh, Zack! Come by! I got you a hot cup of coffee."

I been suspicious of Lillie and her hot cup of coffee. And I know how Abe done out grown that little pen. I got a notion Lil planning on a new pen—and I been too cold to be working on no pig pen. But that cup of coffee sound too good. I feel like it won't do no how to turn Lillie cup of coffee down. But how about the tide? Time and tide ain't going wait and if I don't get them oyster from Goat Island where the money coming from to put grits in them empty children? How I going get thirty-five cent for Junior reading book? And ain't little Evie foots on the ground? While I stand halfting between two opinions, Lil sing out: "Coffee, Zack. Maxwell House. Cow cream and us sugar sack full."

Then when that coffee done drunk, here go Lil: "Oh, Zackie. Before you go, how about fixing old Abe a dry place to sleep? Us'll help. My that pig's a hog now. Been a year since you make us a pen and, Zack, her babies coming and that pen is such a mushy place. Got to be dry and warm for them little young thing when they born in this cold world. If them babies come in that wet, freezing up place in this winter weather, they'll be icicles fast as they're born. Us'll help, Zack. Us'll help."

Gracious crown! It setting in to raining now. What must I do? I can't see Abe little baby coming here in this winter weather and no bed make ready for them. They'll be sure to die. Poor little creatures got to meet a warm bed just same like little humans. If little December pig get too cold their tails will freeze and drop off.

So first news I find myself toting planks most half a mile on my back. Big, old, heavy, heart fat-lighter posts—like so much lead—I have to tote the same way. Then a roll of wire have to come. Digging them post holes I afraid my hand going to pure freeze to that post hole digger. When I cleaning a path through them thick bush and under bush and briar for my wire to run in, I keep thinking about what all Lillie say.

"We going help you, Zack. Us will help."

Cold mist a coming down on me steady and Lil, she in that dry, warm kitchen close by that coffee pot. I can pure smell that Maxwell House. Going help me? And after all them posts buried and that wire about stretched—all done but a few more nail and making a gate— it was getting on towards dark. I can't see so I stop and think: I miss the low tide today. I didn't get one bushel of them oyster. But I know what I can do. I'll catch the low tide tonight and take my gig and go striking. Take my old boat, my old Sinking Sally, and go out night fishing. Might get a bushel of bass and trout. Trout fifteen cents a pound. Then I gone on in the kitchen. Think I'll see what in there before I goes in the creek. Here Lil meets me.

"Zack, how about a hot cup of coffee? More in that pot. Some leave for you. Got us pen ready? Reckon us will have it for Abe to sleep in? You ready for some help. Us'll help you till her in the pen."

I listen. US pen. US'll have it. US'll help.

I say, "No. Got half a day's work to do before that pen ready. Gate to make and trough."

Lil asks (and she do sound too pitiful), "Zacky, you coming back to finish us pen, ain't you?"

That "Zacky" sound too sad. Sometime it "Zack" then it "Zacky."

I tell her I don't know whether I'll make it or not.

But I eat some of Lil's hot hominy and bacon and drink my coffee and gone on in the creek. It happen I hit the tide right and sure enough I did fill my bushel tub with bass and trout. My foots froze up in them cold boots and no socks on and it a freezing, but, man, I have such a time gigging them fish I didn't know I was cold till I hit the house. And I have about four dollars worth of fish. It's sure a pretty sight to see them spotted winter trout a lying so still and cold down there in the oyster rocks and seaweed. And Good Master, I so happy thinking this'll buy grits to keep them children quiet for a week.

After I pull off them boots and wet pants and get myself snuzzled down in bed by Evie, I find out I was cold. Seemed like I couldn't warm up. First news I find myself thinking about Abe's babies coming and the more I study about the cold and them babies coming, the more I know I ain't going have no peace of mind till that pen finished. Evie wouldn't want her young ones coming here and freezing up. And little creature is like little young ones. Them little pig come here and not meet a warm pine straw bed their little tails will freeze and drop off just like I tell you. Then my mind turn to Lil's kitchen. Some way or another she always does manage to have something hot on the stove.

Day clean that old Grandfather rooster started crowing. Seems like he saying, "Get up! Get up! They'll freeze! They'll freeze." So first news I find myself pulling on them boots and heading down to the creek. The first soul I see is Lil. She puts me in mind of one of those little blue darter hawks done got his claw clamped in a little biddy—and me the biddy. Here she got her head stick out the kitchen door and she grinning like a possum. She know the kind of fish I is and the bait I likes.

"Zack! Oh, Zack! Ain't you wants a hot cup of coffee?"

Politics

I've been called the "unofficial mayor of Murrells Inlet," and that hasn't always been meant as a compliment. I don't mind. Either way, I don't. Ever since college I've been interested in politics, and if the Murrells Inlet community was an incorporated town, when I was younger I'd have probably run for the office of mayor until I won it. Politics is about getting people to cooperate and get things done or undone, and the person who leads the group has a lot of say in what's going to happen and how it's going to happen, and I enjoy being one of those people.

Not that being a politician has to be an ego trip. But often it is. Often the power and not the purpose comes to be a person's primary interest, which is unfortunate. But that's not my notion of things, and if I'm thought of as stubborn by others it's just because I've got convictions and I'm not afraid to speak my mind. Well, actually, I might just be a little bit plain old stubborn. I was born under Taurus, the sign of the bull, and I'm called "bullheaded" by my family. Still, stubbornness isn't a bad quality if used for a good purpose. If you're afraid of what people will say about you or that you won't be popular, you might as well not attend the meeting.

It's sad, the apathy that's around today. Grandpapa was a Republican when there were few in this state. But he was a self-made, by-the-bootstraps person and used to making up his mind. He voted for Hoover, which would have been a great embarrassment if anybody had known. Mama had marched with the suffragettes in New York, and Granny was very proud of having the vote even if hers just canceled out her husband's. These days so many people have stopped caring. But I still do, and so do many of my friends.

Murrells Inlet has changed a tremendous amount since I was a girl. We had one little shell-paved single lane on the water's edge, but then the two-lane Highway 17 was paved through the middle of the community and then a giant four-lane bypass got completed. Almost all the little houses and cabins have been replaced with large modern homes, and some have quite grand columns and flourishes. Two restaurants have been replaced with twenty—at least twenty. Still, I have a nice old house on the creek with good trees and a good view of the marsh, and June lives next door. We go swimming with her grandchildren and nieces and nephews in the front yard and paddle kayaks and canoes.

But to the south are seafood restaurants, and during the summer, sixty feet from my house they're blaring out music in the evenings. Plus all the wild and empty beach that we used to look across for a glimpse of the ocean is now crowded with beach houses and even high-rises. Jet skiers are a noisy torment.

Murrells Inlet has changed—actually for the better in a lot of ways but much for the worse in others. It's still a good place to live. I admit that. All the Chandler children have returned here, and we don't begrudge others the same privilege. In fact, I, as a "been here," have many, many friends among the "come heres."

If you walk through a local grocery store these days you might think you're in New Jersey or Ohio—certainly not Murrells Inlet. Last week I met a woman from Connecticut who'd been here nine years. I said, "You're about to become an old-timer. We have so many who came yesterday." But I like these people. So many of them are really contributing a great deal to the community. Many are retired folks who were effective citizens in their old homes and are continuing that here as retirees and bringing a knowledge of cooperation for the common good with them. They don't just come here to play golf, at least not all of them. And our cultural life has improved—concerts, readings. All due to what I call the second invasion. It's good to have money in the community. I can remember when there was none. But it should be obvious to the people moving here that if they don't join us in trying to maintain a good quality of life, what they came here for won't be here any longer.

I'm getting to the end of my story without speaking of our most famous resident, the mystery writer Mickey Spillane. When I was in Germany, his books were literally the favorite reading of the young servicemen. And a man who came from California told me the other day how amazed he was to find himself sitting beside his favorite writer in a South Carolina restaurant. I have to admit those novels are too violent for me, but I heard Mickey speak at a friend's funeral, and it struck me that he had a solid knowledge and understanding of the Bible. And he raised his family here and always took a very active interest in the well-being of this community. I don't know what higher praise you could give to any man—or woman for that matter. Not that Mickey Spillane is a newcomer. Heaven forbid you think that. I guess he's been here more than forty years. What I mean is that he involved himself in what was going on.

Now, my brother Bill still has an oyster lease in the Inlet, and a public oyster ground is located behind the Huntington beach. That's practically unheard of in this age of pollution. The water is clean enough for you to eat the shellfish found in it. We want to keep it that way, and I'm on the Committee for Preservation of the Water Quality under what we call Murrells Inlet 2007. We have a sewer system on Garden City Beach and on the mainland, which means we do have a chance. Bill also heads the boardwalk project for 2007, a marsh-edge walkway that will connect the restaurants and give everyone a good view of the Inlet.

And I should mention the Freewoods Farm Foundation here because I'm on that board. The Freewoods is a giant tract just on the outskirts of the Inlet, on the Horry County side of the line. I'd always thought the name came because runaway slaves went there to hide, but actually it was named by the freed families who bought or were given small pieces of land from their former owners. Then by serving in World War I black men earned enough to enlarge their holdings. They became remarkably good farmers, and the Freewoods Foundation is a group of their descendants. O'Neal Smalls is a law professor at the University of South Carolina, and he's the leader and he put heart and soul into having a forty-acre farm that will be like a museum. They'll show farming with mules and blacksmithing and just what a freedman could accomplish in those hard days of Reconstruction. And because Myrtle Beach is so close, visitors will come.

Gambling. They're trying to bring gambling boats into Murrells Inlet. They'll take passengers out past the three-mile limit, let them gamble, and bring them home—probably broke and more than a little tight. June and I were laughing about our Christian upbringing and this new threat to the Inlet. If we weren't allowed to play cards on Sunday, if we couldn't sew on Sunday, if it was a sin to even thread a needle and sew on a button before church, how could we condone gambling. Well, gambling can be addictive, but gambling isn't a sin. The devil's not involved. This last Sunday I was in Louisville, Kentucky. I went to Churchill Downs and then bet on every horse running, and I made some money. I don't object to gambling on principle. I just think our community and our state has more constructive enjoyments to offer visitors. It looks like the state legislature is about to agree with us and pass a law. But you do have to organize, fight back, and bring such things to the public's attention.

They've built a golf course a little west of here. I've heard they plan to have parking spaces for fifty thousand automobiles. How many square miles of asphalt is that? Myrtle Beach needed a course with that much parking in order to host a big tournament like the Augusta National does. They've come fifteen miles, here near the banks of the Waccamaw River to park fifty thousand cars. Lord, I hope that isn't true.

Oh, yes. And just one little piece of open waterfront is left on our whole stretch, and the owner was threatening to sell it to a restaurant franchise. We kept trying all sorts of negotiations, and finally the County Council came to the rescue and our community has a waterfront park.

And last week the Huntington Beach State Park hosted a meeting of park superintendents from all over the state, and they did enjoy it.

They had fried oysters, roasted oysters, grilled shrimp, fried shrimp, fried fish, and clam chowder. The chowder was superfluous but got eaten anyway.

I made that chowder for my friends at the park, and instead of ending this chapter with a poem or the verses of a song, I'm going to pass on some very valuable political information to you.

Clam Chowder for 125 People

A bushel of clams, 4 heads of celery, 20 pounds of potatoes, and 10 pounds of onions. But we decided to double the potatoes. Then 6 gallons of milk, 4 quarts of whipping cream, and 3 pounds of butter. This was good. Mama used to say she could eat sawdust if she put whipping cream on it. And anytime anybody asked mama about a recipe, she'd say, "Use all the butter you can afford."

Ben Horry. Photograph by Bayard Wootten. North Carolina Collection, University of North Carolina Library at Chapel Hill.

Genevieve Willcox Chandler with Jim and Willy
Peterkin at Lang Syne Farm, Fort Motte, S.C.

Tenant house at Lang Syne Farm, Fort Motte, S.C.

HEATH PIER →

Murrells Inlet in 1954, looking north from Luther Smith's
landing. Photograph by George Morgan.

Luther Smith's landing (land side). Photograph by George Morgan.

Bay Harbor Motel, Highway 17 at Murrells Inlet, early 1940s. Photograph by George Morgan.

Jim Peterkin, a senior in high school

Hurricanes

FOR THOSE OF YOU WHO need refreshing, a hurricane is a tropical storm that usually begins over by the coast of Africa and often ends on our shores. The winds spin counterclockwise at seventy-five miles an hour or better. There's a little eye of calm in the center. Though wind damage can be bad, the most dangerous aspect is the storm surge. A section of the ocean is literally pulled up like a huge bulge, and if this moves on land then the waves come into your living room or over your living room.

Hurricanes are named after people now, but up through the 1940s you just referred to them by the year or by the people killed, as in "the Flagg Storm," which was also "the Storm of 1893." Back when I was a child we didn't have real warnings. You knew the storm was out in the ocean somewhere, but you had to judge by the change in the atmosphere's pressure. If we had a northeaster for three days, then you got that "feel" in the air trouble was coming—or might be. Mama took us away from Murrells Inlet a couple of times. Once for a big storm in 1940 when the wind kept blowing the little Plymouth off the road and we got shelter in a schoolhouse. When we got back home we found mountains of dead marsh grass piled up along the waterfront and out as far as the main creek. Eight to ten feet deep, this floated on the water, and we children were out of the car and running all the way to the edge of this raft. I had a little dog named Toto, after Dorothy's in the *Wizard of Oz,* and he came after me, but his skinny legs went down into the debris and I had to carry him off. I suppose I identified with Dorothy a bit. We certainly had the storms for it.

When Hurricane Hazel struck in the mid-1950s I was running the library over in Georgetown. A bad storm and a few deaths, one of which happened on the street where I was boarding. Even before the water completely receded, I joined the Episcopal priest who lived across the street and walked and waded out to check on our buildings—mine the library and his the church next door. Downed power lines were our biggest danger at that point, but I got to the library and unlocked the door and found water pouring down the inside of every wall. Waterfalls, sheets of water. The library that was the hundred-year-old jail with a flat roof. I'd already had trouble with the drains. I did a foolish thing. I went to the second floor, climbed out the window, got on top of the building, and waded around knee deep pulling the leaves and trash out of the outlets. Thankfully, the building didn't collapse.

That left only the ruined books to consider, and my mother and brothers who were up in Murrells Inlet. I was frantic. The main roads and the phones were out, but then some thoughtful tourists drove a roundabout way and delivered the message that my family members had refugeed in Eason's store and were safe. That afternoon I got home and heard the whole story.

Mama said that she was washing her breakfast dishes and noticed that the tide was full high when it should have been dead low. She knew the water was coming higher and the wind was blowing already. She went upstairs to change out of her housedress, and when she came down ten minutes later the water was across Highway 17 a good hundred yards behind the house. She said this was just a steady rising, no great wall of water but certainly fast.

Now, Mama had a pet coon and a springer spaniel, and she had a violin that she treasured. Grandpapa had bought that last for her in Charleston when she was young, and though she hadn't played in years it was still her treasure. She grabbed the violin, put the pet coon on her shoulder, and with the spaniel swimming beside she waded out in neck-deep water all the way to the far side of the highway. Then she walked a block down to Jimmy Eason's store. The pet coon had already had enough. When she passed a big hickory tree, back in her yard, he sailed off her shoulder, went up the trunk, and she never saw her little coon again. But the spaniel stayed with her, swimming all the way, and she saved the violin. Her house had flooded a couple of feet deep. She lost all those wonderful photographs that Mrs. Bayard Wootten had taken around here and some other things. And the house shifted on the foundation. It would have floated off completely if the big hickories hadn't blocked the way.

And my brother Tommy. He spent most of his life on the water one way or another. My two youngest brothers, Bill and Joe, went on to Houston and worked as engineers in the space program, but Tommy stayed close to the creek. At the beginning of this storm he ran up and down Highway 17 with an outboard picking up people who were stranded. Then it looked like Mr. Herbert Niemeyer was going to lose his party boat, the old *Juniper*. She wasn't but forty-five feet. Still they decided that somebody had to carry that boat out to sea in the middle of the hurricane or it'd be battered to pieces at the dock. Tommy Chandler did it. The water was so high and the waves so high that he crossed completely over Garden City Beach without realizing it. No houses were built straight over from us, and the houses that had been built on the north end were already floating around the inlet. Tommy took the boat through all that across the beach and was in the ocean, which he didn't realize until the weather calmed. Then, not realizing he was in the eye he started in, at which point the wind came back just as bad but from the west, which took him far out to sea. But my brother Tommy made it home with the *Juniper*.

Despite experiences like that you still get complacent about those storms. As the forecasting ability improved over the years the warnings became more and more dire. Murrells Inlet was always being threatened by a tidal wave, it seemed, and yet nothing happened. Once a deputy pulled up in the yard and told us to leave because the destruction would be worse than ten atomic bombs. Well, where were we going in the twenty minutes he gave us? Tommy didn't even get out of bed for that one. He did seem to have good weather sense. And no doubt the officials were exaggerating the danger in order to save lives.

Anyway, I can't say we took the threat of Hugo all that seriously. That was in September of 1989. I was living in a small house right opposite the mouth of the inlet. The water came three feet deep inside my front room, and I lost all these watercolors that Mama had done. And books. I had a collection of South Carolina books that I'd started when I was young—possessions that I had only moved there the year before. Much was lost of a sentimental value, which an insurance adjuster told me was what bothers people the most.

The morning before Hugo hit I was getting ready to hold a meeting. I straightened up the house, listening to the television and thinking, "Those poor folks in Savannah are about to get hit." Then my sister-in-law called from Florida warning me to put Mama's pictures in the attic. I told her we weren't in danger, and when she insisted we were, I said, "If this storm is as bad as you say, my attic won't be left either." So I did nothing to prepare, and when I suddenly had to leave the house, all I did was pick up my new vacuum cleaner and put it on the bed. I saved that vacuum cleaner.

By late afternoon I knew I had to go, but June was recovering from a serious operation, so she couldn't travel far. An old friend invited us to stay in her home across the highway, which seemed safe enough. Tommy was living in this house I'm in—which is strong and high, but he took his wife away from the coast. He was worried about her, but certainly not about himself. I believe he knew by then that the ocean wasn't ever going to harm him. Tommy died of a heart attack four years later.

But on that day June and I parked our cars in a big field behind the inland house we'd been invited to. Eight of us spent the night there. One woman was around ninety and several over eighty, so June and I had pallets on the floor. This house had tremendous live oaks surrounding it, and in the dark we could hear those limbs crack and creak as if to break and all sorts of howling noises. The wind does sound like a train coming down the track. Finally I pulled June's and my pallets under the dining room table. And I didn't sleep that night. About two or three in the morning somebody tried to open the front door and couldn't because of the wind's force. I'm glad they didn't, because the water was within fifteen feet of the house and we'd have been much more frightened knowing the ocean was raging that close.

As I said, I lost Mama's watercolors, but others lost much more. I had a little rental cottage built right on the edge of the creek. Even a full-moon tide threatened it. I felt safe enough myself but warned my tenant Charlie about moving his belongings. The cottage went—totally or almost totally. One little piece of wall was standing. The bathtub was there, but the commode and basin were even gone. One thing I wish I had a picture of: a great big kitchen knife, a butcher knife, had been driven into that bit of cement-block wall. As if a giant had swung down on that wall. And I'd left a wooden bowl out in the yard that actually had pine straw driven into it. You hear about all that, and it's true.

Charlie was in a daze that next morning. He came to me and said, "Sister, I had all my grandmother's silver in that house and it's gone." I said, "Why didn't you put it in the trunk of your car?" Well, he just hadn't, the same as I hadn't raised up the watercolors. Fortunately, he did have a boat at the marina where he could stay. He gave up on his grandmother's silver.

Every day I'd do a little more cleaning up, and about three weeks later I was going along the creek edge at low tide and saw something glinting in the marsh. I bogged out and retrieved a sterling silver goblet. He told me he'd had twelve of those, so I just started digging—clamming for silver—and found ten more. I never found the twelfth. Then about a month later I got a man with a backhoe to take up the remains of the cottage's cement slab. You couldn't put carpet and concrete in the same dump site. So as we were pulling back the carpet, I felt something underneath sort of sliding, and there, where the ocean had hidden them, were the sterling silver trays and the box of table silver. I told Charlie, but he was still in shock and said, "Put them in your attic. I don't want to ever see them again." Eventually he got the silver, but his reaction wasn't so out of the ordinary, for a storm of that nature can affect people on the inside in the same way it wrecks the world on the outside.

That's certainly true of the storm of 1893, the one called "the Flagg Storm," for even now over a century later the Murrells Inlet community lives in its shadow. When Mama was doing her WPA accounts I heard a lot of stories straight from the survivors, and Ben Horry and at least one other told us how young Dr. Ward Flagg had caught a mermaid in a fishnet off of Magnolia Beach and kept this mermaid in a shed. He fed her bread, and she just loved bread. But taking that mermaid out of the ocean was what brought the 1893 hurricane down on us. They talked about her scales and all, which is an incredible story because I really don't think we have mermaids out there in the ocean. Anymore. Perhaps I should add anymore.

So the Flagg family had a house out on the beach. Young Dr. Ward Flagg was there, the one holding the mermaid, and his mother and father, who was Dr. Allard Flagg, and two little girl cousins were visiting from Walterboro, and a number of black servants. Now, a neighbor who had a house on higher ground had sent one of his servants some hours before the storm got bad, inviting the Flagg family and retainers to come over because it was safer. But since old Dr. Flagg had had a dispute with them about land or something, he refused to go or to even send his family and servants. Then when the waves actually got up and really began to lash against the house, they opened the door to let the water wash through. But as the first wave receded, old Dr. Flagg lost his grip at the door, and the suction carried him out to sea. His wife said, "The doctor's gone. I'm going too." Miss Georgie was her name. Then Dr. Ward Flagg, who was a young man, managed to get out of a window at the back of the house and take those two little nieces and one of the servants, Clarissa Horry, with him. These four got on a beach cedar tamarisk whose limbs hung near the house. The limbs of this are willowy and would give, bend without breaking when the water came over. This isn't the common red cedar, which is a stiff and brittle tree, for the foliage is more like a soft fern—not a true cedar but a tamarisk. Dr. Ward Flagg told them all to hold on, which they did even when the waves began to come over them. The limbs would rise above the water and they could catch a breath, and then they'd go down again. Dr. Wardie kept telling the little girls, "Hold on for your mother's sake. Hold on for your mother's sake."

When the storm was over, the people who found Dr. Wardie, his servant, and his nieces had to literally pry their hands loose from the tree. They'd held so tight for so long they couldn't let go. Of course, their clothes had been literally washed away.

Dr. Wardie lived on at Brookgreen until he died in the 1940s. I'm told he never looked at the ocean again. He set up a clinic there and would help people whether they could pay or not. Part of the time my uncle was practicing on Waccamaw Neck as well. They were good friends. By this time Dr. Flagg was being called "Dr. Ward" or "Old Doctor Flagg" or "Dr. Wardie."

When I was young, Mama used to take me to see him, and I thought he was Santa Claus because by then he had snow white hair and a long white beard. He was very kind and gentle. He'd open the door of a closet and give us a peek at the skeleton he kept. Somebody came to see me and said, "Sister you're the only person in the world I've ever seen, except Dr. Ward Flagg, that would let the cat get on the dining room table." My spoiled cat had bounced up on the table. She said, "Dr. Ward's cats slept on the table all the time." Well, that's a compliment of sorts. It's nice to think I've got the doctor's generous nature, and if not, at least we have the cat on the table in common.

For a part of the closing, I'm going back to Mama's WPA records. The ancient Ben Horry gave this account, which has all the rhythm and truth we associate with Gullah stories—almost poetry.

Ben Horry

In 1893 I was working for Ravenel and Holmes and Company in the steamer boat. I was taken up in that storm. Went from Charleston to Georgetown. Generally start the boat at 5 o'clock and not reach Georgetown until nine. We come on breakers and front head of boat went down. And we had to go in the hold and take out all the barrels.

We save five or six different people. One man get his wife to hug the mast. They in a little thing they call life boat. And I coil my line and I let that line fly. If that rope go round your neck and you hold that rope you safe! Another man in a little corn boat. He had his wife and two little children. He had his children roped around the mast. We get his wife then gone back and save the man and trunk. They quit calling me "Ben" then. They call me "Rooster."

After the Flagg storm Colonel Ward take me and Peter Carr, give us a horse apiece and we take that shore to Little River. We found both them children to Dick Pond. Been on Magnolia Beach. Find them close together. Couldn't identify whether this Miss or she daughter-in-law. Right now I got on this shirt got "Ben" written on it. Have no trouble tracing when your clothes got a mark.

One man broke open one trunk, but I didn't care cause I had somebody to my back. Thing you put on your wrist, bracelet, comb for your hair and all in that trunk they find in Myrtle Beach. Such a thing like towel and collar, I find some. Peter find some. Something else. Gracious God! Don't want to see no more something like that. White folks in those times carry poultry and all to beach. Dead horses, dead cow, ox turkey, fowl everything! One Northern woman marry into the Ward family. Dr. Flagg marry in Ward family. Didn't want to acknowledge this lady richer than him. That malice. All his family and children drown out. The Doctor wouldn't go to this lady house. Wouldn't let none of the rest go. He had one woman some-where about Lenwood—Betsy. Kit, Mom Adele drown! Tom Duncan boy, drown! Couldn't identify who loss from who save until next morning! There was kind of an effect like a fog raised by that storm and can't see. If you a servant they can put confidence in they send you where the tornado been. My house wash down from block. Didn't break up.

They fetch old Doctor's body to shore, watch still ticking. I been with the doctor a long time. I been with he Daddy before he born. And when I fetch rice bird he just old enough to take out of my hand. I going tell you what God please with and the Devil hate. I never know him to bother with no woman since he old enough to know what woman was. But he brother! Glory to God, he catch at he own shadow. Glory to God take them all long he path. Didn't pass none. The old Doctor got a life time character with the people he going along with.

That big storm in 1893. Doctor he have enough to make a man study and stop. There all his family—thirteen head—drowned and gone right out to sea. And him and little girl two leave hanging on bush of beach cedar.

After that all bury and gone and Doctor stay in that house a year and don't come out. And I tell you God's truth, that right when the Doctor turn to he toddy. The whiskey keg what he buy would fill this place up to the top! Long as you there, white or colored, he say, "Take a little toddy!"

If we got to Heaven, white or colored, and the Old Doctor not there, I say and John Bunyan say, "It a great wonder!" If I get there and I begin to look around and Doctor not there I think I land the wrong place!

When I was a child that 1893 hurricane had left such an impression on the people who survived it, that like the Civil War it defined who they were. I remember a spiritual being sung. The black people created their music out of experiences in such a vital way, with such straightforwardness. I think about this song all the time and yet I can only remember two of the verses. What I recall is:

> The wind so high, he blow so hard,
> And we ain't know just what to do
> And then we recognize in 'em
> The mysterious power of God.
>
> A hundred bodies come floating by
> And we ain't know just what to do.
> And then we recognize in 'em
> The mysterious works of God.

A Communion

I DIDN'T KNOW UNTIL RECENTLY that the poet Walt Whitman was a homosexual. I mean I'd read half the books on the library shelves and traveled a bit, and still I was mildly shocked to discover this. I guess that kind of innocence comes from being raised more or less as a Southern lady. What I had heard about homosexuality, partly in church and partly out, was that it was a crime against God and nature. I can't say that it occurred to any of us that Jesus would expect us to love all of our neighbors to that degree, but when the AIDS epidemic started I came around—and believe me, I had a far way to come.

A few years back I read in *Time* magazine about Roy Cohn, whom I'd known as a young man when Senator McCarthy sent him to Europe searching for communists. The article said that he was dying of AIDS and that within the next two years, more than likely, every family in the United States would be touched by this fast-spreading disease. I read that, and then in much less than two years a friend's grown child died of AIDS. And at that same time June and I heard through our church about a workshop being given in Charleston where they would train you to help the victims of the illness. People didn't understand and were afraid of even being around AIDS or HIV-positive patients. Even family members were refusing to help—not often but sometimes.

June and I took the workshop, and I'm thankful we did. Once you're educated you understand you're not going to catch anything by driving in a car with someone or just being their friend. We began to drive HIV-positive patients to their hospitals, which was usually a hundred miles or more—Charleston or Durham, North Carolina. These were the two places where all the low-immunity problems could be dealt with. Georgetown County has an AIDs task force, and we're in the care team that works under that.

Judith McNutt, a former Catholic nun who is now an Episcopalian, has been speaking here recently. She believes that God's healing occurs through human love. Unless we can love the unlovable, we can just hang up trying to heal them. This is what God's love is all about. These were the people Jesus often cured with his miracles—the so-called untouchables. But I must admit, working with the care team June and I have been fortunate because all of our patients but one have been very easy to care about. Still, we eventually did have that one who simply wasn't— not because he had AIDS but because of who he was from the beginning, and I must tell you truthfully that it's a hard thing to love that kind of unlovable.

Actually, our very first patient wasn't gay. He'd gotten AIDS from a transfusion in the military, and we would drive him to the Veterans Hospital. He died of leukemia, which he was thankful for—thankful because he didn't want the stigma of an AIDS death affecting his sons. He was thankful for the smallest things—the simplest blessings. He wanted a dog or a cat, but they couldn't be kept there. At the very end of his life a little lizard, a chameleon, got inside the door, and that became his pet. You'd go in the room and the lizard would be on the window beside him or sitting on his shoulder. They knew each other. It may sound silly to some of you, but they touched each other, and that was his comfort.

Another Communion

MY HUSBAND, BILL, DIED JANUARY 17, 1983, and the day before was very cold. Weather permitting, he and I walked the beach every day. And if it was bitter cold, we'd go to Brookgreen Gardens. But this Sunday at lunch he declined the Gardens, saying he'd rather wait until June returned from visiting friends in Charlotte. He and June had grown to be close friends and loved each other dearly. She worked at Brookgreen, and if we waited a day she'd be there to greet us.

Bill had had a heart attack six months earlier and hadn't been well for a good while. I don't know why, but when he declined a walk through the Gardens, I said, "Why don't we go down to St. James—the old brick church on the Santee?" He said, "I'd love it." He picked up the little poodle pup I'd given him recently and we took off—heading back to the semideserted church where he'd proposed marriage twenty-eight years before. We hadn't returned together in all that time.

The sun was shining. No wind. So the cold was easy to bear. We started by wandering about reading the old gray weathered stones and then went inside and sat in a deep dark pew with just the light from the doors and window cracks. And we talked and talked and covered everything that had happened to us since we'd sat there twenty-eight years before. Remarkable. Our son had died in a boating accident six years before, and that last part of our life together had been so hard. We just covered everything, straightened out so much that had been painful, which was such a help to me later. I do have a notion that God guides us on such little journeys—encounters that will leave us with some happy memories—and that memory is one of my best. Bill died the next morning in his sleep.

JIM

Mourning

I'M ASHAMED OF MY ATTITUDE toward Christmas. Since losing my son, Jim, I always want to skip it. A friend asked if I even remember what I was doing last Christmas. I said, "No." I don't, but there's an earlier period in my life when I remember every one—the time when I had my son. That's why it's so painful. You don't know what you might have been doing on, say, the fifth of October or the third of March, but you knew what you were doing on the twenty-fifth of December. That sense of loss never goes away. After Jim died, people would pat me on the hand and say, "Oh, Sister, time will take care of this." And I'd just want to come out with bad words. But after a long time you do react differently to the pain. The pain isn't so severe. Nothing ever changes. Not in your heart. But I think I've done a good job of having compartments in my life. Bill and Jim were both there. Then Bill was there and Jim wasn't there anymore. And Bill died seventeen years ago, so it's almost like I've lived a totally different life since then. Of course, grief isn't a book you can put away. But that first year without my son the pain sometimes was literally physical, as if someone had jabbed me with a knife. So real. Like I could die. You think if you hurt that bad you just have to die. But you don't. You put that pain in a box. You have it in that compartment and you move on.

Jim died by electrocution. He was sailing a catamaran at Cape Hatteras, North Carolina. That was 1977. In June of that year I'd asked him to come to the Inlet. He was working on the farm up at Fort Motte with his half brother and taking classes in horticulture at the local tech school. He was planning to transfer to Clemson University soon but was still uncertain about a major—either horticulture or farming. But in June of that year Bill got very ill from cleaning out his boat, the small cabin cruiser. He'd mixed up some concoction, something real bad, and started spraying for mildew down below. He was ill in no time. But the doctors weren't certain what had happened. At first they thought it was Legionnaires' disease, which had just struck in Philadelphia, but how could that have gotten down here? Anyway, Bill had a very bad lung condition that put him in the hospital in June, and he was still in the hospital when Jim died in September, for in the process of examining him they found he also had prostate cancer. They had to clear up the first illness and then deal with the cancer.

Now, Mama was already bedridden and had been for some years. She was in a wheelchair or the bed, so to provide care for her Bill and I had moved down to the Inlet and were in her house. June was still living in Charlotte and did come every weekend she could, but Mama was my responsibility. With her in bed at home and Bill in the hospital, I had to call Jim. Why did he spend the summer with me? Why did life turn out the way it did? I tried to find someone else to help and had no luck. A pitiful situation. So I told Jim he would have to come, and he did. And besides helping me he started helping my brother Tommy at his restaurant. He washed dishes there at night, which he'd often done when he was younger, and this did give him some contact with the young people he knew from all the summers before. That dishwashing was also his social life, because in the daytime he'd go to the Conway hospital to see his dad. Then he'd come back and sit with Mama while I went to see Bill. We stayed on the road back and forth to the hospital and sitting at bedsides.

At the end of the summer Jim was to return to Fort Motte and the farm and work and study there for another year. Bill was to have his prostate surgery the first week in September. But my brother Tommy and his wife always took their restaurant help on a Labor Day outing— a way of saying thank you. That year they were going to Cape Hatteras, and of course, they wanted Jim to go along.

Tommy had a catamaran that Jim had learned to handle very well. Jim had a smaller sailboat of his own, a dinghy type, that he and Bill had sailed often. Plus, Jim had sailed at the Citadel summer camp for two or three years. He'd sailed in Charleston Harbor and Murrells Inlet, but those were the only places he'd ever sailed. Still, he could handle Tommy's catamaran, so they took it with them on this trip.

Anyway, my brother invited Jim to Hatteras for the whole week, but of course, that wasn't going to be possible. Jim had to sign up for Tech on Wednesday, and Bill's surgery was scheduled for Thursday. Jim could go for just three days. So much was going on, but on our last night together Jim and I did talk. In fact we talked until daylight. We'd been in the same house all summer but hadn't really had a chance to spend time with each other. So that night we covered practically our whole lives together, both bad and good, and it was as if we were summing up and he was launching into his adult years. I'm so glad we had that because what came next was a nightmare.

With Jim going to school, that still left me with the problem of tending to Mama, so on that Monday—Labor Day, in fact—I gave up and decided to put Mama in the hospital until after Bill was recovered. I called her doctor, and he said I should have done this long before. I got the rescue squad to take her over to the Conway hospital, and from there she was to go into a nursing home.

Mama just didn't communicate anymore, and we were soon to realize that this was at least partly due to the combination of medicines she'd been taking. She only had that one doctor, but since she was home he didn't see her often, and it never occurred to me that medicine could be the problem and not the cure. I just assumed that the confusion came from her age and being bedridden so long.

Anyway, I got her to the hospital, and at the admissions desk they said, "Mrs. Peterkin, there's not a bed in the hospital, but your husband is in a double room. Would he mind if we put your mother in with him?" I said, "Well, no. She'd love that." She would too. For much of the preceding spring she hadn't been able to recognize anybody except Bill. She knew him because she'd known him as a little boy. She knew him when she was a teenager and he'd stayed with his grandfather Dr.

Mood, whom Mama loved so. At times when Mama didn't know me, she would know Bill because he was in her childhood. But she didn't know me because I hadn't existed back then. I had to stop calling her Mama during those times. I had to play the nurse and say, "Mrs. Chandler," because if I said "Mama" she got very agitated. In her mind, she didn't have any children. Strange. But I learned to deal with that. And she would always know Bill. So when we rolled her into Bill's room on that Labor Day, she said, "Bill Peterkin, what are you doing here?" She hadn't said any words in ages. Then the funniest thing happened. Everybody on the hall, the nurses and aides, all thought this was Bill's mother, not mine. They said, "You mean he gets along with his mother-in-law like that?" They were amazed that he was so glad to have her there, and for her part, Mama sat up and without help ate lunch from a tray, which she also hadn't done in weeks.

That was on a Monday, Labor Day of 1977. On Tuesday morning Dr. Sasser got a room for her in the nursing home, and I spent that day interviewing people because she still would need around-the-clock supervision. My sister, June, had come down to be with me, and together we found three wonderful women to share the duty of watching Mama. So on that one day things just straightened out. Mama would have care, Bill would have his surgery on Thursday, and Jim would come back to Murrells Inlet that night, go register for school on Wednesday, and have time to return for his father's operation.

June and I left Bill about dark and went back to the nursing home. Mama was agitated, and neither the sitter nor the nurse could quiet her. Mama was all confused again, so I told June I'd lie down with her. I'd been taking care of her so long it seemed simplest for me to handle the situation. I just lay on the bed beside her because in those days I would become mama to her. Then everything worked okay.

I was doing this, and I heard someone open the door and tell June she had a long distance call. After a while Mama got quiet and went to sleep. I thought, "June had a call and she hasn't come back." I left the sitter with Mama and walked down the hall. I went to the front desk and

and saw them down on the edge of the marsh. Jim had been thrown thirty feet from the boat and landed in the marsh. I wish Tommy hadn't told me this. It was a good many years later. He said, "You know, Jim was alive when I got there, and I put my hand on his chest and his heart was beating but there was nobody there." Of course, they called the rescue squad, but Jim died. I had always assumed that he was dead right away.

On top of everything else, that spring somebody in the state legislature was doing a lot of propaganda against capital punishment by electrocution. Articles had run in the paper, and I'd read them all because I had trouble with capital punishment. If I was ever called to a jury with that kind of case, I'd just have to say I can't do it. My husband used to argue that with me. He'd been the foreman of a jury deciding on a man who had shot his pregnant wife in the back while she was running from him. I asked how he could give that man the death penalty? He answered, "How could I not do it?" But no matter what someone had done, I couldn't carry that load, and that attitude had caused me to read all these terrible articles about death from electrocution. I wish I'd never read them.

Bill's surgery was canceled. He was too upset to be operated on. He blamed me for letting Jim go off to Hatteras. He blamed me. He was so devastated they didn't know what to do with him in the Conway hospital, so they sent him down to the one in Charleston. Mama was in the nursing home. I was staying on in our summerhouse because that's where Jim and Bill and I had spent our summers together. I guess I was staying in Mama's house some too, but Jim had never stayed with us there. I guess I was staying in both places. I don't really know.

I remember a Sunday morning finally came when I felt there was no way on earth I could get back in that car and drive to visit Mama and then Bill. We still hadn't told Mama what had happened. At first she was too confused to be told. That was horrible. Going morning and afternoon and never letting her know. She began to think clearer and clearer all the time. The evening that Jim died we thought Mama would die soon and at least we'd never have to tell her. Her doctor, Dr. Sasser, had said, "Miss Genevieve won't be here another month." She lived three more years, but that's because he halted all her medication. Her mind cleared. She was her old self. But then I thought the news of Jim's death would kill her. She'll just die.

But after about six weeks of this torment I was headed down the hall to her room and just started crying. I couldn't go in there. I told the doctor I was going to tell her. "I just can't do this any longer." My stepson came down from Fort Motte and her doctor came and my brother Tommy came, and we were all going to go to the room and tell Mama, knowing that she might die as a result. But we had to. A big water oak tree was right outside of her window. She'd say, "Sis, the tree has lost its leaves so I know it's fall and I know that school has started. I know that Jim has gone back to school, but if Jim Peterkin were in school, he'd come home on the weekends and if he came home on the weekends, he'd come to see me. Now where is he?"

I knew she could be thinking some horrible thing like, "Jim's lying in some hospital half-dead or something." We had to tell her, but when we had all gathered together in the hospital, my brother Tommy took it on himself to walk in ahead of us and tell her. I guess he felt such a sense of responsibility because Jim had been with him. By the time the rest of us stepped in the door, Mama was already sobbing. But Lord, when we entered that room she looked up and cut those tears off just like that. Dr. Sasser said, "Mrs. Genevieve, I know what you're doing. You're singing 'Jesus wants me for a sunbeam.'" I didn't know what he was talking about, but the doctor turned to us and said, "She told me a long time ago that when she was a little girl, if she was ever depressed she sang that."

Mama had a remarkable temperament. She had so many tough times in her life, times when she had to be down, but she never showed it. Mama was always up. Not manic. But I never remember her being depressed. Dr. Sasser said, "When she was little and her spirits got low, she learned to grab the broom and start sweeping the house and singing 'Jesus wants me for a sunbeam.'"

Bill Peterkin

Jim Peterkin in 1977, shortly
before his death

Waccamaw River. Photograph
by George Morgan.

If You Follow Me

Mama was sick and Bill was sick and Jim was dead. Any one of those would have been more than enough to deal with, but put together they seemed next to impossible. God deals with us in funny ways. I remember wishing—not so much thinking I would kill myself, but wishing I could kill myself. I'd have so much rather been dead. There's nothing on earth to live for. Why couldn't I just die? And from that notion I did progress to contemplating how I could take my own life. Not seriously and yet seriously. My gosh, if I'd walked out on Bill and Mama they'd have been left helpless. And yet, I kept thinking how wonderful it would be to do just that.

Of course, having a complete nervous breakdown, the kind where you get to lie down and take some time off, would have helped a lot. But even that was a luxury I couldn't afford—not timewise. I should have gone back and talked with my therapist in Columbia, but it seemed like I didn't have time to do that either. So one bitter cold night during that first winter I decided to just go somewhere and step off a bridge. The hypothermia would get me quick. The water would be cold enough. I wasn't going to do that and yet I was. I was going to get out of this world. I walked out of the house. I was still living alone there. There were no real bridges in Murrells Inlet but maybe I could try Georgetown, try the large span over the Waccamaw River.

I was in such a pitiful state. I was so desperate. I remember how bitter cold the air felt and how I had walked out of the house with no coat or even a sweater. But even the house was cold inside. One of those old summerhouses with no insulation of any kind, but I was staying there to remind me of the time that Jim and Bill and I had spent together. Oh,

I wasn't dealing with things well, not at all. I was dealing with only what I had to deal with. And then standing there in the yard I sort of laughed at myself for having sailed out of the house without even a sweater. How was I going to throw myself off of a bridge into the freezing water if I was too cold to cross the yard to the car? I can understand the quiet desperation that leads people to suicide, but fortunately I couldn't find a really convenient way to take my own life. I was walking along the edge of a field that was beside the house, and finally I laughed out loud and thought, "What a fool I am. What an idiot I am." And then I heard one of those voices you don't really hear. In my head I heard, "If you follow me, remember I'm walking in front." That single sentence turned me around. I forgot about the bridge and went back in the house.

Anger

THIS SEPTEMBER JIM WILL HAVE been dead twenty-two years. He would have been forty-two in August. Last week I went to a County Council meeting where we were discussing the casino boat issue, and I was walking along beside a nice-looking man—one I would call young except he did have a bit of gray hair at his temples. This happens to me occasionally. Not often but occasionally. We happened to be leaving the meeting side by side, and he turned to me and said, "Mrs. Peterkin, you don't know me, but I feel like you're one of the closest friends I have on this earth. Your son, Jim, was my friend." I said, "Gosh, you're getting gray around the temples." My sister, June, was walking beside me too, and she got teary-eyed. But for some reason I was able not to do that. Instead I turned to him and said, "You know, I was so annoyed because somebody sent me a poem when Jim died that said, 'He will be forever young.' I wanted to tell them to go to hell. But you know what that poem said is the truth. I can't look at you and think of you as one of Jim's friends because you are over forty years old and a little bit gray-headed." Jim's friend wasn't put off by this response. Not at all. We had a good chat, and it turned out he'd even been with my son at Hatteras when he died.

People who have suffered loss often do get stuck, though. I don't mean by remembering a loved one as they once were but by not letting go of the anger. I sued the Cape Hatteras Co-op, the one responsible for the sagging power line. My husband, Bill, wouldn't go along with me on that, but I said, "Well, damn it, I'm going to do this whether you think it's right or not." The money didn't matter. Money had nothing on God's earth to do with the suit. Nothing could compensate us for Jim's death, but the sagging power line had been somebody's fault.

A week after Jim's death I actually drove to Cape Hatteras. I knew if I didn't visit the site I would never understand how such an accident could have happened—how Jim could have missed seeing a power line. Everyone kept saying they just came around the bend and that the line couldn't be seen before then, not even from the marina landing. Tommy had left the catamaran up there and told them to give it away or destroy it. He didn't give a damn. He just never wanted to see it again. But I thought of all those young people who loved sailing, and they would all quit. Of course, that's true, but that shouldn't have been my concern right then. I wasn't in my right mind, I know. But I told Bill's doctor and Mama's nurses that I was driving to Hatteras, and I went. One of the girls who was on the boat with Jim went with me, and I took my brother's pickup to haul the boat trailer. I drove all night to Cape Hatteras and got there in the morning. I had to see for myself. I never would have understood. The people at the motel were so kind. They tried to make me stay so I could get some sleep. But I wouldn't. We arrived as the sun was rising. You couldn't see the line from the landing. There was no sign anywhere warning of a power line. And the power line was sagging badly. I got the boat hitched up and drove straight back home.

There should be a sign at the marina warning boaters. I came home thinking they needed at least that. Meanwhile a friend suggested we sue the power company and gave me the name of a lawyer, one who happened to have worked with Jim in the church's youth group and who considered my son a friend. Bill thought that horrible to even talk about, but I felt that was the only way I could make them raise the power line and put up a sign. Of course, the money couldn't replace our son, but the lawyer had to build his case that way. What would Jim's earnings have been if he had lived a normal length of life. Oh, all that turned me off so. Terrible.

Still I would lie awake at night thinking that I could kill the people responsible, the people in the electric co-op, whom I had never laid eyes on in my life. That I wanted them dead because they were responsible for my son's death. I realize this was totally irrational. I mean, I even realized this as I was having the thought. All I can say is, time does take care of that kind of anger.

My lawyer thought I made a mistake. But the co-op finally did mount a sign, one bigger than a large refrigerator, and they put poles way higher than had ever been in that part of the country and raised the lines way higher. They made certain that kind of accident couldn't happen again, and when they did I settled out of court for a small amount.

They did what I'd asked. Not quickly. This didn't get done until after my husband, Bill, had died, which was six years later. And though I hate to think such, perhaps without the threat of a suit, they would have done nothing at all. Oh, my lawyer had a case. If we'd continued he would have won. The young people hadn't been drinking or doing drugs. The kids were straight, and nobody saw the line. We could have easily won, but the co-op had finally done what I asked. Anger is a part of life, and often a useful part. Angry people are capable of accomplishing great good. But I couldn't let those feelings keep me awake every night for the rest of my life. I was right to let the matter drop.

An Afterlife

DURING THOSE DARKEST DAYS OF grieving I ended up eating out. I'd go to some little place I'd never been and have a meal. If I went to a grocery store I could only think of things that Jim liked to eat. I couldn't make myself buy anything, except I would pick up a big bag of chocolate, those Hershey kisses, the little silver-wrapped bells. I kept those by my bed. I bet I ate enough chocolate to make a normal person diabetic. Some years later I read that chocolate is a good antidepressant and that people often treat themselves the way I had without knowing it. I would eat the kisses all night long and read all night long. I couldn't sleep. When the sun rose I could go to a little place at Surfside, a restaurant on the dock, and watch the ocean.

I did have comforts in my life. Protections. I had gotten over my notions of suicide and heard the voice telling me, "If you follow me, remember I'm walking in front." That certainly was a good comment on free will and on the path God expected us to take in this life. How much freedom does He give us? Enough, I suspect. But in the final say, He is walking in front. I had that to reassure me, and of course, I had the consolation of Jim's dream. When he was about fourteen he had dreamed of sailing on that strange two-hulled boat with the bright sail. He'd dreamed of leaving the boat and entering a banquet hall and taking a seat at the table, and at the opposite end of the table had been the king, who was Jesus Christ. "The land I had come to was so much more beautiful than the land I left." That's what my son had told me back then.

His death did reaffirm my belief in immortality. As I mentioned, my mother-in-law, Julia, and my husband were deeply spiritual people in a sense. But they both found conventional forms of worship and beliefs amusing. They'd laugh at what they considered my naive notions. And yet those very notions were a simple reality for Lillie. I remembered her beliefs. I remembered the strength and warmth with which she and Zacky and so many others had approached both this life and the next. I remembered her singing that "Heaven is a beautiful place." I had all that from them. I had Jim's dream of entering heaven, of being at the welcome table. I remembered Mama's courage. And at that point I had a dream of my own—one that also helped me to survive.

In this dream I was out on the beach, the same beach that's across the marsh from the Inlet. Only the beach was like the beach I knew as a child. There were no buildings. Just a bare, desolate beach, empty except for me, who was out there, and I was feeling this extreme loneliness. I felt so alone. I knew Jim was gone. Still, the wind was coming from the south. A beautiful day, at least out over the ocean. The ocean was sparkling and a wonderful shade of blue with little whitecaps. No big rolling waves. The wind out of the south so those little whitecaps were rolling right toward me. And I saw someone swimming. This person seemed to be swimming toward me. I started walking out into the water, and I saw that the swimmer was Jim. He stood up right in front of me, but he—well, he wasn't like Brookgreen's gilded statue, the golden Dionysus. No. When I was young and in Paris I saw the Folies-Bergère. Those dancers were naked, buck naked, but they were gilded. They looked like statues—and yet they were human. And that's how my son looked. He wore nothing, and he was glowing. His face looked so happy. He just stood up in front of me and smiled at me and said, "Mom, swim hard for yourself from now on. You don't have to swim for me anymore."

Mother's Day

ON THE MOTHER'S DAY BEFORE that last summer, Jim came down to the coast for the weekend. He was helping on the farm at Fort Motte but came to the Inlet and brought me a hanging basket with a beautiful fern. And he said, "Mom, I'm carving something for you. It's a little sailboat on a cedar limb, but I didn't get it finished, so I'll bring that present to you later." Well, he died in September, and our house at the farm stayed vacant after that. I didn't even visit after his funeral. I had Mama to watch, and anyway, I couldn't face that house.

The next Mother's Day that came around, though, I suddenly felt like I had to go to the farm. I don't know why. I just took off and left June and Bill with Mama. I went early that Sunday morning, the morning of Mother's Day. I drove up to the farm and went in the house. Even today I can't deal with that house very well. I went in and was wandering around and crying because in those days that's all I could do when confronted with such memories. Finally, I sat down in the den. By then it was a little after noon. The sunlight was coming in the window and hit the mantel. I looked up, and there was this little carving resting in the light on the mantel. I picked it up and studied the inlay—a sailboat cut into a strip of cedar limb.

I looked on the back, and the inscription read, "I love you too."

A Final Word

Dogs and Flowers

THIS LAST STORY BEGINS WITH Mama's retirement—which occurred some years before Jim's death. You see, Mama had kept working at Brookgreen Gardens until she was seventy-three. In a way she was already in heaven, surrounded by the beauty of that garden. But she really was too old. So early one Monday morning I drove to Myrtle Beach and brought back watercolor paper, watercolors, and brushes. Monday being her day off, I said, "Mama, paint me a picture." She hadn't held a brush in forty-five years, but she went out by the creek and painted two watercolors, which she then left on the dining room table. A friend came by and insisted on buying one. Mama kept insisting they were "nothing." But I said, "Forty-five dollars," because that's what the materials cost. He handed her the money and took the painting. Oh, I wish I had that one back.

After that Mama couldn't wait until her days off to be painting and would even go down to the creek edge when she got home after five. Soon she retired and painted full-time. She had a one-person exhibit at the Columbia museum and within two years was making more than she'd made at Brookgreen, and she went on painting until her last year.

Her other passion was flowers, one she'd always had, of course. The other day one of the members of her old garden club told me of a flower show in Georgetown. Mama was at Brookgreen and they picked her up on the way. All the women had their special arrangements, and the cars were all filled with flowers and containers. She said, "Your mama came out of that garden with a Pepsi-Cola bottle full of water. We said, 'Mrs. Genevieve, where are your flowers?' She said, 'Oh, I'll gather them on the way.' She knew the wild orchids were blooming, so every few minutes she'd holler 'Stop the car! Stop the car!' She got yellow-fringed orchids and all sorts of beautiful wild orchids that nobody else would even notice on a ditch bank. She won a prize with her arrangement.

As far as I know the arrangement was in the Pepsi bottle, and that was an easy story for me to believe. When we took Mama up to Fort Motte to stay with us, that drive from the Inlet would take a good two and a half hours if you didn't stop. We couldn't stop every time she saw a wildflower. We did stop some. But on one trip when Bill was going in a separate car, I said, "Mama, we're going to leave early, and I already have buckets of water in the car." We came down a back way, through the forests, and every time she yelled "Stop the car!" I stopped. Jim and his cousin Rhett jumped the ditches and picked the flowers. The trip took six and a half hours, but we arrived with two big buckets filled with wildflowers. And she so loved painting pictures of those.

I can't imagine Mama in a heaven that has no flowers. For that matter, I can't imagine myself in one without flowers either. What's a heaven without dogs and flowers?

I suppose I read that phrase somewhere long ago, but if it's a quote I don't know from where. It's mine now, but not a totally Christian concept, I'm afraid—at least not a traditional white Southern one.

We children always had a dog cemetery at the Hermitage, a place off close to the water, but it couldn't be seen because of all the shrubbery. I remember one of the crash boat crew, a Czech who spoke with a strong accent, had a dog that got hit by a car. He was just standing there crying, and Mama came up in her car. She said, "Come with us." She let him bury his dog in our cemetery, which did help some. Anyway, all these graves had little white crosses on them, and other members of the crew buried dogs and we ended up with quite a little yard of white crosses off in the woods.

One day Miss Susan Alston came to visit, and she and Mama were taking the path to the creek and I was tagging along behind. Miss Susan spotted those crosses and asked, "Genevieve, Genevieve, what cemetery is that?" And Mama answered, "Oh, the children have buried their dogs there." And Miss Susan was horrified. She pointed at the crosses and practically shouted, "You've let them make Christians out of them."

You see. It takes the innocence of children to get dogs into heaven. Except thinking back on the Heaven's Gate New Year's service, I can see where adult faith can accomplish the same thing. There in that dark church the congregation had the horses and cows bow down to the baby Jesus in the manger. Oh, dogs are in heaven. I don't have a bit of trouble, not a bit, imagining our son, Jim, off in one of heaven's green meadows. He's finished his meal at the welcome table and he's running in this meadow. A beautiful lake is nearby and all through the grass wildflowers are blooming, and one of our old dogs is running up to join him.

What could heaven be if dogs weren't allowed in? All pets? Some would say horses, and the horses did bow down. I say dogs and cats and, of course, birds. And the birds can be wild. The metallic green and gold Carolina parakeets have got to be up there for Julia. And the clapper rails, which for me are just poor old marsh hens, are slipping through heaven's marsh grass. Sandpipers are pecking the sands on the edge of heaven's ocean. And indigo buntings like we had up at Fort Motte—buntings are a must. When Mama came to visit and saw those she'd just start screaming. A whole flock of them, just a great maze of color, would come up out of the hedgerows. Fish? Those dolphin leaping in the sparkling water of heaven's Gulf Stream.

What could heaven be to be more beautiful than what we have here? But perhaps I'm wrong. Maybe it is all golden streets and cities. Though it's hard for me to imagine heavenly cities.

Well, one thing I'm certain of, and that's God's love. The kind of love we experience down here on this earth, whether it's a parent's love for a child or husband to wife, sister to brother, or friend to friend, is what's waiting for us in the hereafter. That's God's greatest gift to us—this hint of what's to come. The nearest we get to understanding His love for us is by considering our love for others. The dogs and flowers are just a bonus.